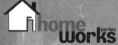

home
works series

SOME
ASSEMBLY
REQUIRED

INSTRUCTIONS *for* AN AMAZING MARRIAGE

BY TOMMY NELSON

SERENDIPITY
HOUSE

GROUP DIRECTORY

Write your name on this page. Pass your books around and ask your group members to fill in their names and contact information in each other's books.

Your Name: _____

Name: _____	Name: _____
Address: _____	Address: _____
City: _____	City: _____
Zip Code: _____	Zip Code: _____
Home Phone: _____	Home Phone: _____
Mobile Phone: _____	Mobile Phone: _____
E-mail: _____	E-mail: _____
Name: _____	Name: _____
Address: _____	Address: _____
City: _____	City: _____
Zip Code: _____	Zip Code: _____
Home Phone: _____	Home Phone: _____
Mobile Phone: _____	Mobile Phone: _____
E-mail: _____	E-mail: _____
Name: _____	Name: _____
Address: _____	Address: _____
City: _____	City: _____
Zip Code: _____	Zip Code: _____
Home Phone: _____	Home Phone: _____
Mobile Phone: _____	Mobile Phone: _____
E-mail: _____	E-mail: _____
Name: _____	Name: _____
Address: _____	Address: _____
City: _____	City: _____
Zip Code: _____	Zip Code: _____
Home Phone: _____	Home Phone: _____
Mobile Phone: _____	Mobile Phone: _____
E-mail: _____	E-mail: _____
Name: _____	Name: _____
Address: _____	Address: _____
City: _____	City: _____
Zip Code: _____	Zip Code: _____
Home Phone: _____	Home Phone: _____
Mobile Phone: _____	Mobile Phone: _____
E-mail: _____	E-mail: _____
Name: _____	Name: _____
Address: _____	Address: _____
City: _____	City: _____
Zip Code: _____	Zip Code: _____
Home Phone: _____	Home Phone: _____
Mobile Phone: _____	Mobile Phone: _____
E-mail: _____	E-mail: _____

Some Assembly Required: Instructions for an Amazing Marriage
© 2005 Tommy Nelson

Published by Serendipity House Publishers
Nashville, Tennessee

ISBN: 1-5749-4217-4

Dewey Decimal Classification: 306.8
Subject Headings:
MARRIAGE \ HUSBANDS \ WIVES

Unless otherwise indicated, all Scripture quotations are taken from the
Holman Christian Standard Bible®,
Copyright © 1999, 2000, 2002, 2003 by Holman Bible Publishers. Used by permission.

Scriptures marked NASB taken from the *New American Standard Bible®,* © 1960, 1962, 1963, 1968, 1971, 1972, 1973, 1975, 1977, 1995 by the Lockman Foundation. Used by permission.

To purchase additional copies of this resource or other studies:
ORDER ONLINE at www.SerendipityHouse.com;
WRITE Serendipity House, 117 10th Avenue North, Nashville, TN 37234
FAX (615) 277-8181
PHONE (800) 525-9563

1-800-525-9563
www.SerendipityHouse.com

Printed in the United States of America
11 10 09 08 07 06 05   1 2 3 4 5 6 7 8 9 10

CONTENTS

Welcome to Community!

Meeting together with a group of people to study God's Word and experience life together is an exciting adventure. A small group is ... *a group of people unwilling to settle for anything less than redemptive community.*

Core Values

Community:
God is relational, so He created us to live in relationship with Him and each other. Authentic community involves *sharing life together* and *connecting* on many levels with the people in our group.

Group Process:
Developing authentic community requires a step-by-step process. It's a journey of sharing our stories with each other and learning together.

Stages of Development:
Every healthy group goes through various stages as it matures over a period of months or years. We begin with the *birth* of a new group, deepen our relationships in the *growth* and *development* stages, and ultimately *multiply* to form other new groups.

Interactive Bible Study:
God provided the Bible as an instruction manual of life. We need to deepen our understanding of God's Word. People learn and remember more as they wrestle with truth and learn from others. The process of Bible discovery and group interaction will enhance our growth.

Experiential Growth:

The goal of studying the Bible together is not merely a quest for knowledge, but should result in real life change. Beyond solely reading, studying, and dissecting the Bible, being a disciple of Christ involves reunifying knowledge with experience. We do this by bringing our questions to God, opening a dialogue with our hearts (instead of killing our desires), and utilizing other ways to listen to God speak to us (group interaction, nature, art, movies, circumstances, etc.). Experiential growth is always grounded in the Bible as God's primary means of revelation and our ultimate truth-source.

The Power of God:

Our processes and strategies will be ineffective unless we invite and embrace the presence and power of God. In order to experience community and growth, Jesus needs to be the centerpiece of our group experiences and the Holy Spirit must be at work.

Redemptive Community:

Healing best happens within the context of community and in relationship. A key aspect of our spiritual development is seeing ourselves through the eyes of others, sharing our stories, and ultimately being set free from the secrets and the lies we embrace that enslave our souls.

Mission:

God has invited us into a larger story with a great mission. It is a mission that involves setting captives free and healing the broken-hearted (Isaiah 61:1-2). However, we can only join in this mission to the degree that we've let Jesus bind up our wounds and set us free. As a group experiences true redemptive community, other people will be attracted to that group, and through that group to Jesus. We should be alert to inviting others while we maintain (and continue to fill) an "empty chair" in our meetings to remind us of others who need to encounter God and authentic Christian community.

Sharing Your Stories

The sessions in *Some Assembly Required* are designed to help you share a little of your personal lives with the other people in your group as you learn to build an amazing marriage. Through your time together, each member of the group is encouraged to move from low risk, less personal sharing to higher risk communication. Real community will not develop apart from increasing intimacy of the group over time.

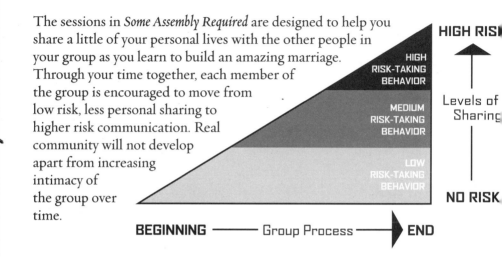

Sharing Your Lives

As you share your lives together during this time, it is important to recognize that it is God who has brought each person to this group, gifting the individuals to play a vital role in the group (1 Corinthians 12:1). Each of you was uniquely designed to contribute in your own unique way to building into the lives of the other people in your group. As you get to know one another better, consider the following four areas that will be unique for each person. These areas will help you get a "grip" how you can better support others and how they can support you.

G – Spiritual Gifts: God has given you unique spiritual gifts (1 Corinthians 12; Romans 12:3-8; Ephesians 4:1-16; etc.)

R – Resources: You have resources that perhaps only you can share, including skill, abilities, possessions, money, and time (Acts 2:44-47; Ecclesiastes 4:9-12, etc.)

I – Individual Experiences: You have past experiences, both good and bad, that God can use to strengthen others (2 Corinthians 1:3-7; Romans 8:28, etc.)

P – Passions: There are things that excite and motivate you. God has given you those desires and passions to use for His purposes (Psalm 37:4,23; Proverbs 3:5-6,13-18; etc.)

To better understand how a group should function and develop in these four areas, consider going through the Serendipity study entitled *Great Beginnings*.

GROUP MEETING

Each of your group meetings will include a four-part agenda.

1. **Breaking the Ice:**
This section includes fun, uplifting questions to warm up the group and help group members get to know one another better, as they begin the journey of becoming a connected community. These questions prepare the group for meaningful discussion throughout the session.

2. **Discovering the Truth:**
The heart of each session is the interactive Bible study time. The goal is for the group to discover biblical truths through open, discovery questions that lead to further investigation. The emphasis in this section is on understanding what the Bible says through interaction within your group.

To help the group experience a greater sense of community, it is important for everybody to participate in the "Discovering the Truth" and "Embracing the Truth" discussions. Even though people in a group have differing levels of biblical knowledge, it is vital that group members encourage each other share what they are observing, thinking, and feeling about the Bible passages. Scripture notes are provided at the end of each session to provide additional Bible understanding.

3. **Embracing the Truth:**
All study should direct group members to action and life change. This section continues the Bible study time, but with an emphasis on leading the group members toward integrating the truths they have discovered into their lives. The questions are very practical and application-focused.

4. **Connecting:**
One of the key goals of this study to lead group members to grow closer to one another as the group develops a sense of community. This section focuses on further application, as well as opportunities for encouraging, supporting, and praying for one another.

BONUS – Taking it Home:
Between each session, there is some homework for group members. This simply includes either a question to take to God or a question to take to your heart, as well as a date night for each couple. These experiences are designed to reinforce the content of the session and help couples strengthen their marriages.

Stages of Group Life

Each healthy small group will move through various stages as it matures. There is no prescribed time frame for moving through these stages because each group is unique.

Birth Stage: This is the time in which group members form relationships and begin to develop community.

Multiply Stage: The group begins the multiplication process. Members pray about their involvement in establishing new groups. The new groups begin the cycle again with the Birth Stage.

Growth Stage: Here the group members begin to care for one another as they learn what it means to apply what they have discovered through Bible study, shared experiences, worship, and prayer

Develop Stage: The Bible study and shared experiences deepen while the group members develop their gifts and skills. The group explores ways to invite neighbors, friends, and coworkers to meetings.

 **Subgrouping:** If you have more than 12 people at a meeting, Serendipity House recommends dividing into smaller subgroups after the "Breaking the Ice" segment. Ask one person to be the leader of each subgroup, following the "Leader" directions for the session. The Group Leader should bring the subgroups back together for the closing. Subgrouping is also very useful when more openness and intimacy is required. The "Connecting" segment in each session is a great time to divide into smaller groups of 4 to 6 people.

GROUP COVENANT

As you begin this study, it is important that your group covenant together, agreeing to live out important group values. Once these values are agreed upon, your group will be on its way to experiencing true Christian community. It's very important that your group discuss these values—preferably as you begin this study. The first session would be most appropriate.

* **Priority:** While we are in this group, we will give the group meetings priority.

* **Participation:** Everyone is encouraged to participate and no one dominates.

* **Respect:** Everyone is given the right to his or her own opinions, and all questions are encouraged and respected.

* **Confidentiality:** Anything that is said in our meetings is never repeated outside the meeting without permission.

* **Life Change:** We will regularly assess our progress toward applying the "steps" to an amazing marriage. We will complete the "Taking it Home" activities to reinforce what we are learning and better integrate those lessons into our marriages.

* **Care and Support:** Permission is given to call upon each other at any time, especially in times of crisis. The group will provide care for every member.

* **Accountability:** We agree to let the members of our group hold us accountable to commitments we make in whatever loving ways we decide upon. Unsolicited advice giving is not permitted.

* **Empty Chair:** Our group will work together to fill the empty chair with an unchurched person or couple.

* **Mission:** We agree as a group to reach out and invite others to join us, and to work toward multiplication of our group to form new groups.

* **Ministry:** We will encourage one another to volunteer and serve in a ministry, and to support missions work by giving financially and/or personally serving.

I agree to all of the above_____ date: _____

Meeting Planner

The leader or facilitator of our group is _____ .
The apprentice facilitator for this group is _____ .

We will meet on the following dates and times:

	Date	Day	Time
Session 1	_____	_____	_____
Session 2	_____	_____	_____
Session 3	_____	_____	_____
Session 4	_____	_____	_____
Session 5	_____	_____	_____
Session 6	_____	_____	_____

We will meet at:

Session 1 _____
Session 2 _____
Session 3 _____
Session 4 _____
Session 5 _____
Session 6 _____

Childcare will be arranged by:

Session 1 _____
Session 2 _____
Session 3 _____
Session 4 _____
Session 5 _____
Session 6 _____

Refreshments will be arranged by:

Session 1 _____
Session 2 _____
Session 3 _____
Session 4 _____
Session 5 _____
Session 6 _____

SOME ASSEMBLY REQUIRED INTRODUCTION

Some Assembly Required is the premier small-group study in Serendipity's HomeWorks marriage and family series. Marriage and family are not old, irrelevant ideals. *Home still works!*

A lot of people tend to think marriage is whatever a society decides it is. They admit that marriage was needed in the past. The unique marriage partnership between a man and a woman created families. Family units gave structure to societies. People knew who they were because they belonged to families.

Many people feel the time has come to change the ground rules for marriage. In the modern world, family ties have weakened. Many believe that marriage is losing its grip on our culture. The number of couples getting married has declined dramatically, while the rate of divorce has soared. Many couples who marry now live together first. Increasing numbers of couples cohabitate and parent children without ever getting married. Too many children grow up with only one parent.

The Bible, however, teaches that marriage began in the heart and mind of God when He created Adam and Eve. Marriage isn't a social convention we can discard in favor of "other arrangements." It's tied up with being created in the image of God. We were created to enjoy the kind of harmony, interdependence, and intimacy experienced between the Father, the Son, and the Holy Spirit.

Marriage takes work, but it's worth the effort. The Bible is God's instruction book for developing an amazing marriage, one that works as He designed it. As you participate in this study, you will connect with other couples while at the same time strengthening your marriage relationship. You will discover invaluable truths as you interact with other members of your group around the six steps for creating an amazing marriage. You'll explore:

* How marriage was designed to work
* Becoming a loving leader
* Becoming a courageous completer
* How to speak your wife's love language
* How to speak your husband's love language
* Marriage modeled by a unique biblical couple

This unique study will be a lot of fun, but it will also take you on a life-changing journey if you take the marriage assembly instructions to heart. Enjoy the ride!

A Marriage Made in Heaven?

HOW IT'S DESIGNED TO WORK

Almost everybody brings high expectations into marriage and dreams of happy days to come. You find that woman or man who makes your heart sing, and you can't imagine any discord in the days ahead that can't be made right with a kiss and a hug. In fact, you can't imagine any discord. After reality sets in, it's hard to imagine that anyone ever believed the adage, "Marriages are made in heaven."

In this study, we'll walk through six steps in the *Instructions for an Amazing Marriage*. Step #1 this week focuses on understanding how God designed marriage to work.

Breaking the Ice 15 MINUTES

LEADER: Be sure to read the introductory material in the front of this book before the first session. To help your group members get to know one another better, have each person introduce him or herself and then take turns answering all of the "Breaking the Ice" questions.

1. Which classic Elvis song reminds you of your marriage? Why?
   - ○ "You Ain't Nothing but a Hound Dog"
   - ○ "Love Me Tender"
   - ○ "Heartbreak Hotel"
   - ○ "I'm All Shook Up"
   - ○ "I Can't Help Falling in Love with You"
   - ○ Other: _____ .

2. If you received premarital counseling, what was your reaction to it? Why?
   - ○ Nobody every told me we could get premarital counseling.
   - ○ Oh, please. Who needs counseling? We're in love!
   - ○ Man, this counselor's marriage must not be much fun. We'll never have these problems.
   - ○ Whoa! I never thought of some of these things. Maybe we're not as ready as we thought.
   - ○ Wow! This is helpful. I'm glad we got this counsel.
   - ○ Other: _____ .

3. Did you have any unrealistic expectations you brought into your marriage that now cause you to you shake your head and chuckle? Please explain.

 # Discovering the Truth 20-25 MINUTES

LEADER: In each section of "Discovering the Truth," ask various group members to read the Bible passages. Be sure to leave at least 15 minutes for the "Connecting" segment at the end of your time together.

Most of us are living right in the center of the "reality" stage of marriage. Every marriage has its difficulties and struggles. We may have a "match made in heaven," but some conflicts get hot enough to suggest a far different place of matrimonial origin. In time most couples come up with their own way of getting along. Some are happy. Some are resigned to so-so relationships. Some live with regular tension or a distant tolerance for one another.

The Bible, however, teaches that marriage began in the heart and mind of God when He created Adam and Eve. It's tied up with being created in the image of God. The Master Design that He has in mind for husbands and wives is the kind of harmony, interdependence, and intimacy experienced between the Father, the Son, and the Holy Spirit.

In the Beginning God Created ... Marriage

26 Then God said, "Let Us make man in Our image, according to Our likeness ...

27 God created man in His own image, in the image of God He created him; male and female He created them.

28 God blessed them; and God said to them, "Be fruitful and multiply, and fill the earth, and subdue it; and rule over the fish of the sea and over the birds of the sky and over every living thing that moves on the earth."

GENESIS 1:26-28 (NASB)

[7] Then the LORD God formed the man out of the dust from the ground and breathed the breath of life into his nostrils, and the man became a living being.

[8] The LORD God planted a garden in Eden, in the east, and there He placed the man He had formed. [9] The LORD God caused to grow out of the ground every tree pleasing in appearance and good for food, including the tree of life in the midst of the garden, as well as the tree of the knowledge of good and evil. ...

[15] The LORD God took the man and placed him in the garden of Eden to work it and watch over it.

[16] And the LORD God commanded the man, "You are free to eat from any tree of the garden, [17] but you must not eat from the tree of the knowledge of good and evil, for on the day you eat from it, you will certainly die. [18] Then the LORD God said, "It is not good for the man to be alone. I will make a helper who is like him." ... [21] So the LORD God caused a deep sleep to come over the man, and he slept. God took one of his ribs and closed the flesh at that place. [22] Then the LORD God made the rib He had taken from the man into a woman and brought her to the man. [23] And the man said:

This one, at last, is bone of my bone, and flesh of my flesh; this one will be called woman, for she was taken from man. [24] This is why a man leaves his father and mother and bonds with his wife, and they become one flesh.

GENESIS 2:7-9, 15-18, 21-24

LEADER: Discuss as many discovery questions as time permits. The strongest application questions appear in "Embracing the Truth." It will help to highlight in advance the questions you don't want to miss.

Be familiar with the Scripture Notes at the end of this session to help clarify any issues. There are additional tips in the Leader's Notes section that begins on page 88.

1. How does the passage in Genesis highlight that God's nature is three persons (Father, Son, and Holy Spirit) in relationship? How does God's creation of humanity reflect the "image of God"?

2. The Hebrew word translated "helper" in verse 18 occurs 20 times in the Old Testament. In all but four instances (Genesis 2:18, 20; Isaiah 30:5; Daniel 11:34), it refers to God coming to rescue or coming to the aid of humanity. The word "helper" never refers to the help of a subordinate, but rather carries the meaning of "completing" and "rescuing." How have you witnessed wives giving this kind of "help" to their husbands?

3. In what way should knowing that each of us is created in the image of God affect the way we treat our spouses?

God did not make Adam and Eve at the same time. God made Adam first. He put the man in a place of delight, the garden of Eden. God and the paradise He created met all of Adam's emotional, physical, and spiritual needs. This "child" was well taken care of. As with a literal child, God did not just give Adam everything. He didn't spoil him. God made Adam work.

Then Genesis 2:18-24 describes God's creation of a "helper" for Adam. Both Adam and Eve were handcrafted by God, both reflected God's glory, and both were God's image-bearers. But there *were* distinctions between them. Adam was designated as the leader and protector. Eve was designated as the helper—the one who would complement and complete Adam. Adam was completed by Eve, and Eve by Adam.

STEP #1:
Follow the Manufacturer's Design Specifications

The Apostle Paul highlighted the specifications for a successful marriage in many of his letters to churches. The first letter to the Corinthians is one of these; it clarifies how the roles of husband and wife were designed to work in marriage. Marriage is the context for which these verses were intended.

² Now I praise you because you remember me in all things and keep the traditions just as I delivered them to you. ³ But I want you to know that Christ is the head of every man (husband), and the man (husband) is the head of the woman (wife), and God is the head of Christ.

1 CORINTHIANS 11:2-3

4. As you grew up, where did you first hear someone claim, "The husband is the head of the home"?

   ○ John Wayne movies
   ○ My father
   ○ Sermons at church
   ○ Listening to groups of men talk
   ○ Other: _____

5. If a man won't let Christ be his head, how do you think that affects his ability to be a servant-leader for his wife?

6. The Greek word for headship refers to "source" or "origin," not to "superior rank." In what sense do you think the Bible means "the man is the head of the woman"? On what occasions might a women take on some leadership in an area of the marriage?

7. How can we carry out this biblical teaching and maintain mutual respect and honor in the context of marriage?

In 1 Corinthians 11:2-3, Paul reaffirms that God's design of unity within diversity in marriage is based on what God is like within the Trinity. Father, Son, and Holy Spirit are equal as Persons, but have different roles. God the Father exercises a leadership role over God the Son, who provides direction for God the Spirit. Husbands and wives also are equal as persons, but have different roles. The men, for their part, must submit to the Son (to whom they obviously are not equal).

The truth is, a man is not the sovereign in his home. Christ is. A husband isn't free to behave any way he wants. He is accountable to Jesus. To be a good husband, a man first has to live out the implications of being the bride of Christ. He isn't ready to lead until he understands and acknowledges the servant-leadership of Christ.

 # Embracing the Truth 10-15 MINUTES

Making STEP #1 Work

LEADER: This section focuses on beginning to integrate what group members have learned from the Bible in their own marriages ... where "the rubber meets the road."

Problems emerge in marriages when husbands and wives ignore what God teaches in Genesis about how men and women complete one another. That great philosopher Rocky Balboa, in the 1976 movie *Rocky*, clearly described his relationship with his wife-to-be (Adrian) saying, "She's got gaps. I got gaps. Together, we fill gaps." Communication problems, sexual problems, affection problems, and leadership problems pop up as soon as men stop leading in love and women stop responding with respect.

There's a sense in which marriage is like a friendly tennis game. You both have to play, and you should play cooperatively rather than competitively. You want to keep the volleys going a long time. It's a lot easier for a wife to be respectful to a kind husband and for a husband to be kind to a respectful wife. If a wife is respectful and a husband is kind, you probably will have a successful marriage.

8. What do you tend to do when things don't go the way you want in your marriage?
   - ○ I withdraw and sulk quietly.
   - ○ I simmer until the pressure reaches a boiling point.
   - ○ I blow up and vent all over the place.
   - ○ I physically leave for a while.
   - ○ I get even some way sooner or later.
   - ○ Other: _____ .

9. What is a practical step you could take to become a better "tennis player" in your marriage?

10. What would have to change in your thinking and your emotions for you to take this step?

 **Connecting** 15 MINUTES

LEADER: Use "Connecting" as a time to begin to bond with, encourage, and support one another. Invite everyone to join in and to be open with one another, but allow members who don't wish to share on a particular topic to pass.

As a group, we have a unique opportunity to bond as friends for the life of this study, and to share in a spiritual adventure that could transform our marriages and our relationships with God. Use this set of questions to deepen your knowledge of one another and start to connect at the heart level.

1. Take turns around the group briefly sharing how long you've been married, where you got married, and where you went on your honeymoon.

. Tell about a time earlier in your marriage when you failed to apply God's design for your role in marriage—where you were a poor tennis partner. What happened? How did you come to realize your problem? Do you do things differently now?

EADER: Be sure to get the ball rolling on the social event—see item 3. 'ou'll finalize these plans next session.

lso, take some extra time in this first session to go over the group ages at the front of this book. Now would be a great time to pass round your books and have everyone fill out contact information in the Group Directory at the very front of each book.

. Brainstorm a social activity your group could do. Consider having dinner together, going to a movie or concert, having a game night, hiking or cycling, etc. The possibilities are endless, depending on the interests of the group. You'll finalize your plans during your next session.

Record group prayer requests in the space below. In addition to specific prayer equests, pray together for each person individually, that he or she would recognize reas of adjustment required to better fulfill the roles God has given for marriage.

Prayer Requests:

Taking it Home

You will benefit from these lessons in proportion to how much effort you put into them. Before you meet together for Session Two, spend time in two activities designed to stimulate your inner life and your marriage relationship.

(1)   A Question to Take to Your Heart on page 23

(2)   A Date Night on page 24

When? _____   Where? _____

SNEAK PEEK

Next time we meet, we'll focus on how men need to lead in their homes.

A Question to Take to Your Heart

Ask your heart the following question. Be brutally honest with yourself. During the next session, there will be opportunity to share any key insights you feel comfortable sharing with the group. However, it's always okay to pass.

Refer to your answer to Question 8 in "Embracing the Truth" about how you tend to respond when things don't go your way.

✢ Why is that my coping skill of choice? What does use of that coping technique say about what I really believe? What's behind my way of handling difficulties?

DATE NIGHT

Get out your wedding and honeymoon photo albums and look through your pictures together. In the course of your conversation, be sure to share the following points with one another. During the next session, each couple will share one fun and one meaningful memory with the group.

✦ What was your funniest memory from your wedding or honeymoon?

✦ How did your families live out roles in marriage? How did your parents' approaches square with what God says, and with what you want in your marriage?

✦ Ask each other, "On a scale of 1 (poor) to 10 (great), how am I doing at living out God's design for my role as a husband or wife? Where do we need to adjust?"

To close your "Date Night," take each other's hands and pray for each other as you strive to live out your roles and complete each other.

SCRIPTURE NOTES

Genesis 1:26-28; 2:7-9, 15-18, 21-24

1:27 male and female. Who of us is not aware of the differences between men and women? And yet, both were created in the image of God and given the responsibility to take care of the earth. In how men and women relate to each other, we are different; in how we relate to God, we are the same.

1:28 rule. God gave mankind the responsibility to rule over the world. Ruling over and subduing does not mean merely "being the boss" nor is it an invitation to exploitation. Instead, mankind's "rule" over the world means nurturing it with creativity and care.

2:7 formed. God made humanity. The complexity and the miracle of the human person is God's handiwork. The word "formed" pictures a potter working with clay. We owe to God the wonder of our bodies, minds, and souls.

2:15 work it and watch over it. In God's plan, He gave to humanity the role of working and guarding His creation as they functioned in the role of stewards. This is as true today as when the responsibility was first announced and understood. This is why, no matter what our task, we should say, "What does God require of me here, in this place, now?"

2:18 not good for the man to be alone. God made Adam in need of someone to complete him. One of the reasons for this was the practical matter of procreation. God is a creative God. He created the plants with seeds to procreate. He created a man and then a woman to bring children into the world.

2:22 made the rib ... into a woman. If God had made Eve from the dirt as a totally separate being, it might have been easy for man to treat her like dirt. But God didn't. He made her from the flesh and bone of Adam's side. She was his body. Thus the idea of Christ loving the church as His body (Eph. 5:23) finds its way all the way back to the garden of Eden.

2:23 woman ... taken from man. In Hebrew "man" is *ish*; "woman" is *ishah*. *Ishah* is not derived from *ish*, but it sounds like it. Biblical Hebrew was a poetic language. Its speakers and writers loved word plays, so it said that *ishah* was taken out of *ish*. Adam and Eve understood the implications of that.

2:24 leaves ... and bonds. From the beginning of creation, God established the order of the family. Just as Eve was made from Adam's own body, so when a couple is married the two become one. A man leaves his home, the roots from which he came, and establishes a new life with his new family. Even though polygamy was practiced in Old Testament times, it is clear from this verse that God's plan was for a man and a woman to become one in lifelong service and union.

1 Corinthians 11:2-3

11:3 God is the head of Christ. Paul applied the doctrine of the Trinity to marriage. Within the Trinity there is order. Paul wrote, "Christ is the head of every man, and the man is the head of the woman, and God is the head of Christ." Christ deferred to His Father. A man must defer to Christ if he expects a woman to defer to him. Notice that there's equality among the Persons of the Trinity. Father, Son, and Holy Spirit are equal in eternal personhood, glory, holiness, and immutability. "Head" refers to "source" or "origin," not "superior rank."

Follow the Leader

BECOMING A LOVING LEADER

In the first session of *Some Assembly Required* we completed Step #1 for creating an amazing marriage: *Follow the Manufacturer's Design Specifications*. We began by looking at the relationships of the Father, Son, and Holy Spirit within the Trinity. We then considered how God created man and woman as people of equal worth with different roles. In conclusion, we saw that both the relationships within the Trinity and within marriage are characterized by equality and order, by unity in diversity.

During this session, we will explore the husband's unique role in marriage. Step #2 lays out the job description for the head of the home, and it may surprise us.

 **Breaking the Ice** 15 MINUTES

LEADER: The "Breaking the Ice" questions will help group members get better acquainted and begin talking casually about the session topic. Keep the tone of the conversation light and be sure everyone gets a turn.

1. In your opinion, which of these sitcom husbands is the best role model, and which is the worst? Explain your choices.

   ○ Ricky Ricardo from *I Love Lucy*
   ○ Al Bundy from *Married with Children*
   ○ Cliff Huxtable from *The Cosby Show*
   ○ Ward Cleaver from *Leave it to Beaver*
   ○ Ray Barone from *Everybody Loves Raymond*
   ○ Other: _____

2. As you were growing up, what man in your extended family best exemplified committed, loving leadership in his marriage? What impressed you about him?

In the "Taking it Home" section at the end of Session One, you were asked to take a question to your heart, and to look at and discuss your wedding and honeymoon photos. Hopefully you enjoyed reminiscing and gained some fresh insights.

. How did your "Taking it Home" activities go? Would you share a key insight from your heart about how you handle difficulties, or from your "Date Night" discussion on living out your roles?

 # Discovering the Truth 20-25 MINUTES

STEP #2 – Love Your Wife the Way Jesus Loves the Church

Husbands, love your wives, just as also Christ loved the church and gave Himself for her, [26] *to make her holy, cleansing her in the washing of water by the word.* [27] *He did this to present the church to Himself in splendor, without spot or wrinkle or any such thing, but holy and blameless.* [28] *In the same way, husbands ought to love their wives as their own bodies. He who loves his wife loves himself.* [29] *For no one ever hates his own flesh, but provides and cares for it, just as Christ does for the church,* [30] *since we are members of His body. ...* [31] *For this reason a man will leave his father and mother and be joined to his wife, and the two will become one flesh.*

EPHESIANS 5:25-31

And the man said: This one, at last, is bone of my bone, and flesh of my flesh; this one will be called woman, for she was taken from man. [24] *This is why a man leaves his father and mother and bonds with his wife, and they become one flesh.*

GENESIS 2:23-24

LEADER: Discuss as many discovery questions as time permits. The strongest application questions appear in the "Embracing the Truth" section. It will help to highlight in advance the questions you don't want to miss.

Familiarize yourself with the Scripture Notes at the end of this session to help clarify any issues. There are additional tips in the Leader's Notes section that begins on page 88.

1. What are some practical ways that a husband can love his wife the way Christ love the church?

2. When men are on the road and get hungry, they pull over and feed their bodies. When their fevers rise, they reluctantly go see the doctor. They take care of what their bodies need. How will husbands treat their wives if they love them as their own bodies?

3. What common threads do you see in the Ephesians 5:25-31 and Genesis 2:23-24 passages? How are they linked? Consider the connection between husbands and wives, as well as a husband's responsibility.

   The word for "love" in Ephesians 5:25 is not *eros*. Paul wasn't writing about erotic love. It is not *phileo*, the term for brotherly companionship. It's *agape*, which refers to personal sacrifice for the good of the beloved. It's a decision to act in loving ways regardless of passing emotions. A husband should love his wife as Christ loved the church—giving himself up as he focuses on loving her. That's the standard—the bar we need to reach for that is set by Jesus!

   Men, it's clear that loving your wives as your own bodies goes all the way back to the creation of woman. Eve was Adam's flesh and bones—she came from his body. In the same way, those who believe in Christ as their Savior become His body. When a man and a woman marry, they become united as "one flesh" to the depths of their souls. A man who loves his wife as his own body, echoes the glorious creation story, revisits his wedding vows, and portrays Christ's love for His church.

Love Her Intentionally

Husbands, in the same way, live with your wives with understanding of their weaker nature yet showing them honor as co-heirs of the grace of life, so that your prayers will not be hindered.

1 PETER 3:7

4. Which of these statements do you think *best* explains what Peter meant when he referred to the "weaker nature" of women? Why?

   ○ Women are generally physically weaker than men are.
   ○ Women are generally psychologically more delicate than men are.
   ○ Women accept a vulnerable position when they submit to men.
   ○ Women tend to be nurturers while men tend to be defenders.
   ○ Other: _____ .

5. In what ways do husbands struggle with "understanding" their wives? In what ways do they struggle to show them honor as "co-heirs of the grace of life"?

6. What are some ways you've observed men being good students of their wives—leading "with understanding"?

   Peter instructed husbands to be students of their wives, to be in the know about them. When he referred to "their weaker nature," he wasn't saying women can't handle the hard knocks of life. They obviously can. Peter taught husbands to regard their wives as fine china, crystal, or porcelain. Men are not to handle their wives recklessly. They are to treat their wives gently, and especially treasuring them when they accept the vulnerable position of submission.

   "The grace of life" in this passage embraces all the meanings of the noun "life." Husbands and wives are co-heirs of *physical* and *emotional* life through creation and of *spiritual* life through their relationship with Jesus. They share the same level of dignity in life. When husbands treat wives as co-heirs, they recognize that in Christ "there is no Jew or Greek, slave or free, male or female; for you are all one in Christ Jesus" (Galatians 3:28).

Embracing the Truth

Making STEP #2 Work

Lead Her with Character

2 Oh, that he would kiss me with the kisses of his mouth! For your love is more delightful than wine.
3 The fragrance of your perfume is intoxicating; your name is perfume poured out. No wonder young women adore you.

SONG OF SONGS 1:2-3

There are three components to leadership in marriage. The first is *recognition*. The man is the recognized leader. A husband should be respected because he is a man under the authority of God. For his part, he must submit to God before he can lead his wife well.

The second component of leadership is *character*. Men are to lead on the basis of admirable character. Song of Songs 1:2-3 records the heroine's praise of her beloved. Chief among the things she loved about him was his good "name" that was "intoxicating" for her. In biblical terms, a man's "name" is his character. The strength of his name is in direct correlation to his relationship with God.

The third component of male leadership is *direction*. A man should seek direction from God and share it with his wife. From the beginning God has expected the husband to lead in studying the Word of God. When a woman has to harangue a stubborn, unruly man and drag him off to church, something is wrong. The husband is supposed to lead.

7. What are some practical ways that a husband can lead from a good "name" (Songs 1:3)?

8. In Session One, we discussed how women were created to be "helpers"—strong, capable completers for their husbands (Genesis 2:18-24). How can a woman demonstrate that she recognizes and respects her husband's leadership?

. In our culture, the concept of male leadership has come under fire, so men have often become passive and domesticated. In your opinion, how should a husband set the tone in his marriage, as God has instructed him in Ephesians 5:25-30?

0. As husbands seek to live out Ephesians 5, how might women encourage their husbands to lead in marriage and follow Jesus' example?

 **Connecting** 15 MINUTES

It's easy to feel threatened by God's standards for both husbands and wives. We eed to affirm one another as we attempt to put tough biblical teaching into practice. 1 this session we have a chance to give "attaboys" to the men in our group.

Focus on the men in the group one at a time. As a group (men and women), share a total of 2 or 3 loving characteristics or leadership qualities you see in each man.

Men, go around the circle and take turns telling the group about a character quality you want to exhibit in your life as you mature in Christ. Explain why this quality is important to you.

3. Finalize plans for the social activity you discussed in the first session. Decide the kind of event, its location, and its date and time.

Record group prayer requests in the space below and pray regularly for them between now and the next session. Take time now to pray specifically for the men in your group that God would develop in each one the character quality he said he wanted to develop in Question 2 of "Connecting."

Prayer Requests:

 # Taking it Home

Rejoice in God's truth. He wants to set you free, not burden you. He wants to see you grow and develop into all you can be, not restrict you and cramp your style. Before the next session, schedule a time to talk with God and a time to enjoy and interact with your mate.

1) A Question to Take to God on page 34

2) A Date Night on page 35

You will have the opportunity share key insights during the next session.

When? _____   Where? _____

SNEAK PEEK
Next time we meet, we'll focus on the unique role
of being a godly wife.

A Question to Take to God

When you ask God a question, expect His Spirit to respond to your heart and spirit. However, don't manufacture an answer. Don't write down what you think the "right answer" is. Don't dig through the Bible looking for an official statement. Just pose the question to God and wait on Him. Be sure to record what you hear from Him; you will accelerate your growth as you keep a journal of the insights you gain from your times with God.

✦ Men ask God: "What barriers in my life are preventing me from loving and leading my wife the way You want me to?"

✦ Women ask God: "Is there anything holding me back for encouraging my husband to be the leader in our home?"

DATE NIGHT

Men, this activity rests entirely on your shoulders as a loving leader for your wife. Before the next session, take your wife on a date. There are three stipulations. First, choose an activity both of you will enjoy. Don't play the martyr and take her to the ballet if you hate it. Second, make it a goal to surprise her—at least a little. Don't do the same old thing by grabbing a pizza at some place with big-screen TVs tuned to a ball game. Third, ask her out formally, as though you were courting her. Use your imagination to make this evening feel special. While on your date, do the following:

✢ Men share a couple of key things with your wife that you genuinely appreciate about her.

✢ Ladies share a couple of key things with your husband that you admire and respect about him.

To close your "Date Night", when you get home, hold hands and pray together. Husbands thank God for His blessings on your life together. Wives ask God to guide your husbands as the loving leader for your family.

SCRIPTURE NOTES

GENESIS 2:23-24

2:23 woman ... taken from man. In Hebrew "man" is *ish;* "woman" is *ishah. Ishah* is not derived from *ish,* but it sounds like it. Biblical Hebrew was a poetic language. Its speakers and writers loved word plays, so it said that *ishah* was taken out of *ish.* Adam and Eve understood the implications of that.

2:24 leaves ... and bonds. From the beginning of creation God established the order of the family. Just as Eve was made from Adam's own body, so when a couple is married, the two become one. A man leaves his home, the roots from which he came, and establishes a new life with his new family. Even though polygamy was practiced in Old Testament times, it is clear from this verse that God's plan was for one man and one woman to be joined together in lifelong service and union.

SONG OF SONGS 1:2-3

1:2 he ... his. Solomon is typically assumed to be the lover in this song. *love.* In Hebrew the noun (which is in the plural denoting intensity) refers to divinely blessed sexual love. Delight is experienced in various physical expressions of love (v. 4; 4:10; 7:12; Prov. 7:18; Ezek. 16:8). *your love is more delightful than wine.* This is echoed by the chorus in verse 4. The lover returns the compliment in 4:10.

1:3 your name is perfume poured out. Literally, "your name is emptied oil." In biblical days the oil produced by the first pressing of a batch of olives was used in temple worship because it had no impurities. The second pressing was used in food preparation. The last pressing contained a lot of pulp and was used for soap. The clarified oil of the first pressing burned bright and smokeless in the temple lampstands. It made incense and ritual ointments of highest quality. In Hebrew, "name" and "perfume" sound similar. *adore.* Unlike the word used in verse 2, this Hebrew word refers to romantic feelings.

EPHESIANS 5:25-30

5:25 love your wives. This is the main thing Paul said to husbands. It is so important that he repeated this injunction three times (vv. 25,28,33). Paul urged a type of love: *agape,* which is characterized by sacrificial, self-giving action. *just as also Christ loved the church and gave Himself for her.* Two qualities characterized Christ's actions on behalf of the church: love and sacrifice. The husband is called upon to act toward his wife in the same way.

5:27 to present the church. At a Jewish wedding, the bride was presented to the groom by a friend.

5:28 their own bodies. Eve was Adam's flesh and bones—she came from his body. Believers in Christ are His body. When a man and a woman marry, they become "one flesh" (Gen. 2:24; Eph. 5:31). The man's deep-rooted instinct to care for himself should carry over to his wife.

Peter reminded husbands that the respect they are to show to all people (2:17) is also due to their own wives. *in the same way.* Peter harkened back to the example of Christ who voluntarily gave Himself for the sake of others (2:21). *their weaker nature.* Literally, the "weaker vessel." There has been much debate as to what this means. It could refer to anatomical differences between men and women (this phrase was used in Greek to refer to the woman's body), to the inferior position of women in that society, or to the comparative lack of physical strength on the part of the woman. While all these are true, the key message is that women accept a more vulnerable position when they submit to their husbands. *showing them honor.* Literally "assigning honor." This statement is an intentional paradox. In the Greco-Roman culture women were treated as an inferior class and inferiors honored their superiors. Christ, in stark contrast taught leaders to serve those they led (Matt. 20:25-26). *co-heirs.* Both husbands and wives are equal participants in the grace of God, again reinforcing the idea that men and women have equal value in God's eyes.

R-E-S-P-E-C-T

BECOMING A COURAGEOUS COMPLETER

During our second session, we began to get a handle on Step #2 for creating an amazing marriage: *Love Your Wife the Way Jesus Loves the Church.* We noted that God expects husbands to be loving and intentional servant-leaders in their homes *after* they have learned to submit to His authority. A loving husband leads with the welfare of his wife and children in mind rather than his own selfish interests.

During this session, we will explore the wife's unique role in marriage. Step #3 focuses on how a woman comes alongside her husband and completes him—through respecting, helping, and following his lead.

Breaking the Ice   15 MINUTES

LEADER: The "Breaking the Ice" questions will relax people and help them continue to connect better with one another. You aren't looking for "right" answers, but rather for viewpoints with which group members have grown up.

1. In your opinion, which of these sitcom wives is the best role model, and which is the worst? Explain your choices.
   - ○ Lucy Ricardo from *I Love Lucy*
   - ○ Peggy Bundy from *Married with Children*
   - ○ Clair Huxtable from *The Cosby Show*
   - ○ June Cleaver from *Leave it to Beaver*
   - ○ Debra Barone from *Everybody Loves Raymond*
   - ○ Other: _____

2. What typically comes to mind when women hear the phrase "submit to your husband"?

3. As you were growing up, what woman in your extended family respected her husband in the most positive way? What impressed you about her?

LEADER: Encourage each person to share a key insight from "A Question to Take to God" or the "Date Night". This should only take a couple of minutes each, but allow a little more time if someone has something inspiring to share. Affirm husbands who made special efforts to surprise their wives.

4. How did your "Taking it Home" activities go? What was one memorable moment?

Discovering the Truth   20-25 MINUTES

STEP #3 – Respect Your Husband's Leadership

LEADER: In each section of "Discovering the Truth," ask a group member to read the Bible passage. Be sure to leave at least 15 minutes for the "Connecting" segment at the end of your time together.

22 Wives, submit to your own husbands as to the Lord, 23 for the husband is head of the wife as also Christ is head of the church. He is the Savior of the body. 24 Now as the church submits to Christ, so wives should [submit] to their husbands in everything.

EPHESIANS 5:22-24

1. In what ways is it risky for women to submit to their husbands?

2. It is clear from this passage that God intends for wives to submit to their husbands. Do you think the way wives express submission should be similar from marriage to marriage, or do you think it should express itself differently depending upon the couple? What is best and why?

3. What do you think should be the common elements of submission in all marriages?

4. In Ephesians 5:21, Paul directed all Christ-followers to treat one other with respect and to submit to one another in the fear of Christ because they recognize the image of God in the other. How can this view of dignity coexist with maintaining the roles God has set up for husbands and wives?

That command for wives to submit to their husbands troubles many and angers others because women reasonably fear being taken advantage of. What did God have in mind when He spoke of submission? We can use two thoughts to define it. One is *respect* and the other is a *willingness to follow*. A submissive wife recognizes that God has given her husband a position of leadership. That is respect. When she responds positively to his leadership, she shows a willingness to follow.

We've discussed that God's design for marriage involves working together cooperatively—respecting and treating each other with dignity, just as Jesus does. Before a woman decides to marry and submit to a man as her husband, she should observe whether he is mature, whether he follows God, and whether he can handle the responsibility of being a husband. Only then should she choose to place herself under his leadership.

Once a woman marries, it takes courage on her part to submit to her husband's leadership. However, her submission creates the arena in which his leadership operates and develops. God gives a man a wife to complete him and to create a unit that is stronger than either of the individuals are alone.

What Does Submission Look Like?

Then the LORD God said, "It is not good for the man to be alone; I will make him a helper suitable for him."

GENESIS 2:18 (NASB)

3 In the same way, older women are to ... encourage the young women to love their husbands and children, 5 to be sensible, pure, good homemakers, and submissive to their husbands, so that God's message will not be slandered.

TITUS 2:3,5

1 Wives, in the same way, submit yourselves to your own husbands so that, even if some disobey the [Christian] message, they may be won over without a message by the way their wives live, 2 when they observe your pure, reverent lives.

1 PETER 3:1-2

5. What is a "suitable" helper? In what ways might a wife complete and complement her husband?

6. What positive impact do you think the example of a submissive wife can have on each of the following?

○ Marriages in her neighborhood

○ The unbelieving society at large

○ Her children

○ A husband who believes in and follows Christ

○ A husband who *does not* believe in and follow Christ

7. Why should older women be the best source of information about what submission to one's husband really means? What have you learned from older women about loving your husband and respecting him?

8. When a woman submits to her husband, she trusts him to lead in a way that has her best interests at heart. As soon as doubt and fear enter the emotional picture, trust disappears. How can a husband build his wife's hope and trust? How can a woman have hope for the future regardless of how her husband leads?

Husbands are commanded to love their wives in the same sacrificial way that Christ loves the church. When wives submit to their husbands, they have reason to hope their submission has practical, spiritual value. Their submission is a service to the Lord (Colossians 3:18). It meets a standard set by God at creation. Wives' submission casts a good light on the message of God (Titus 2:5). Amazingly, it makes the strongest possible appeal to the heart of any husband who disobeys God's Word (1 Peter 3:1-2).

For a wife to exercise trust in her husband, she must have hope for a positive future. This hope must be founded in the Lord who empowers her to submit hopefully to her husband regardless of her situation. Remember, her submission is not in any way passive. If a wife is to be a suitable helper she must stand at her husband's side, give him her insights, gently encourage him, and at times, challenge him to step up to be God's man.

Embracing the Truth

10-15 MINUTES

Making STEP #3 Work

LEADER: This section focuses on helping couples begin to integrate what they have learned from the Bible in their own marriages.

Reversing the Curse

As the result of Adam's and Eve's sins in the garden of Eden, God gave the following curse among several others, which has been passed on to all generations of men and women. God described the devastating consequences sin would produce in human nature and human relationships.

He said to the woman: I will intensify your labor pains; you will bear children in anguish. Your desire will be for your husband [to rule over or control him], yet he will dominate you.

GENESIS 3:16

9. What is the result of the fall of humanity into sin and how does it play out in our marriage relationships?

10. "Desire" and "dominate" are both negative words in this passage about the consequences of sin. God told Cain, "Sin is crouching at the door. Its *desire* is for you, but you must master it" (Genesis 4:7). In these two passages in Genesis, "desire" denotes a passion to control. Why do you think wives want to control their husbands? Why do husbands tend to dominate their wives?

43

11. A true Christian marriage redeems our relationship from the curse. What changes does God's Spirit have to make in us to transform us from controllers to courageous completers and from dominators to sacrifical leaders?

As a result of humanity's original fall from glory in the garden, people don't trust one another. They guard themselves. Accordingly, wives don't want to submit to their husbands. They feel a need to protect themselves, and therefore desire to control their husbands.

Sin prompts husbands to distrust their wives. They feel that if they lead sacrificially they could be taken advantage of. Consequently, husbands tend to dominate their wives. Immature, insecure husbands can be violent in their domination. God knows marriage is tough at times, but He wants men and women to realize they absolutely need Him to redeem and transform them before they can expect to succeed in marriage. A man must lead rightly and a woman must desire rightly for the marriage to flourish.

 **Connecting** 15 MINUTES

When we think about the impact of sin on our ability to build open, unselfish relationships in marriage, it's easy to get discouraged. We could end up thinking we have to settle for marriages marred with conflict and scarred by petty grudges and resentments. We need to take every opportunity we have to encourage one another and to let the Lord transform us from the pattern of the world around us into the glorious image He intended.

1. This week, focus on the women in the group one at a time. As a group, (men and women), share a total of 2 or 3 ways you have seen each woman support and encourage her husband.

2. Women, go around the circle and take turns telling the group about a character quality that you want to exhibit in your life as you mature in Christ. Explain why this quality is important to you.

3. What are some areas of concern in your marriage that this group can pray for and encourage you?

LEADER: One at a time, have each couple sit inside the circle of the group while everyone else lays hands on them and prays briefly for God's blessing on their marriage.

Record group prayer requests in the space below and pray regularly for them between now and the next session.

Prayer Requests:

 # Taking it Home

It is important to remember that submission to God and to one another is expected of all believers in Jesus, not just married women (Ephesians 5:21). A woman who isn't submissive in other areas of life won't submit in her marriage. A man who isn't submissive in other relationships won't know how to receive his wife's submission or graciously meet her desires when needed and appropriate. Before Session Four, use these activities to give you insight into how submissive your spirit is.

(1) A Question to Take to Your Heart on page 47

(2) A Date Night on page 48

When? _____   Where? _____

SNEAK PEEK

Next time we meet, we'll look at 10 practical ways husbands can love their wives. Husbands, you don't want to miss this one!

A QUESTION TO TAKE TO YOUR HEART

Look into your heart for the answer to the following question. This is introspection time—time to grapple with what drives your thinking and behavior, with what you believe in the deep recesses of your heart about God, yourself, and your spouse. Be sure to record your thoughts.

✠ Women ask your heart: How do I feel about God asking me to submit to my husband? Does this raise the rebel in me? Or, do I use His command as an excuse for being a doormat? What might my emotions reveal about what I really believe about God, my husband, or myself?

✠ Men ask your heart: How might I subtly or even subconsciously dominate my wife? Most women don't resist submitting to Christ's leadership, so how can I make it safer and easier for my wife to submit to my leadership?

DATE NIGHT

Until your next small-group session, it's "Submit-to-Your-Spouse Season." You'll find two coupons below, one for you and one for your spouse. Each of you should use one to request a favor of the other. You don't have to fulfill both requests on the same day. Submit to one another's requests according to these rules:

1) Don't request anything that costs more than $25.00, requires more than three hours of time, or asks your mate to do something disagreeable to him or her.
2) Do ask for something you will truly enjoy.
3) Fulfill your mate's request with his or her enjoyment in mind.
4) When you thank your wife or husband for lovingly submitting to you, be face-to-face and make eye contact.

You may not have done both of these "Date Nights" activities on the same day. If not, hold hands and pray after each of them. The one served should pray, emphasizing the current concerns of the other.

ONE "SUBMIT TO YOUR SPOUSE" COUPON

I _____ request that my spouse _____
honor me by _____
_____
_____

I submit this request on _____ It needs to be fulfilled by _____
I agree to reciprocate.

I love you! Signed _____

ONE "SUBMIT TO YOUR SPOUSE" COUPON

I _____ request that my spouse _____
honor me by _____
_____
_____

I submit this request on _____ It needs to be fulfilled by _____
I agree to reciprocate.

I love you! Signed _____

SCRIPTURE NOTES

GENESIS 2:18

not good for the man to be alone. God made people to need each other. One of the reasons is the practical matter of procreation. God is a creative God. He created the plants with seeds to procreate. He created a man and then a woman to bring children into the world. He also brought man a "helper like him" that could stand by his side to complete and complement him.

GENESIS 3:16

desire will be for your husband. "Desire" and "dominate" are both negative words in this passage about the consequences of sin. In Genesis 4:7, God told Cain, "Sin is crouching at the door. Its desire is for you, but you must master it" (Genesis 4:7). In these two passages in Genesis, "desire" denotes a passion to control.

EPHESIANS 5:21-24

5:21 submitting to one another. In the context of Ephesians 5, one of the key aspects of being filled with the Spirit involves mutual submission within the Christian community. This applies regardless of the relationship or status within those relationships: acquaintances, business associations, friendships, family, and even people we don't know.

5:22 submit. This injunction from Paul must be understood in its historical context. In Jewish law, a woman was a "thing," not a person, and she had no legal tights. In Rome, too, divorce was easy and women were repressed. Against this, Paul proposed a radical, liberating view: (1) wives were called upon to defer only to their husbands (and not to every man); and (2) submission was defined and qualified by Christ's headship of the church (Christ died for the church). The husband was to love, sacrifice for, and serve his voluntarily submissive wife. *to your own husbands.* A woman owes submission only to her husband, not to all men (as first-century culture taught).

5:23 Christ is head of the church. This is a headship of love, not merely authority; of nurture, not of suppression.

TITUS 2:3-5

2:3 teach what is good. Formal instruction was not exclusive of an older woman's modeling "what is good" for younger women in terms of a woman's accepted social role of the day as a wife and mother.

2:5 submissive to their husbands. Paul was not placing women under the authority of all men. Instead he had in mind voluntary submission to the woman's own husband.

1 PETER 3:1-2

3:1 in the same way. By this phrase Peter made a transition from slaves to wives. Just as the behavior of Christ was the model for slaves, so too it was for women. *submit yourselves.* "Submit" translates the Greek word *hupotasso*. *Hupotasso* is compounded from *hupo*, the preposition meaning "under," and *tithemi*, the common Greek verb "to place." *Hupotasso* denoted that a woman voluntarily placed herself under her husband's leadership. *won over.* Peter (like Paul) did not counsel Christian women to leave unbelieving husbands. His desire was that the husbands eventually be converted.

Speaking Your Wife's Love Language
HOW TO SUCCEED IN LOVING YOUR WIFE

Last time we progressed to Step #3 in creating an amazing marriage: *Respect Your Husband's Leadership*. God asks women courageously to accept a position in marriage that leaves them vulnerable. However, when a wife embraces her role as her husband's completer and helper, she both urges him on and provides a picture of the divine relationship to a watching world.

In Session Four, we will swing our focus back to husbands and how they can express their love for their wives in meaningful and practical ways. Pastor and author Stu Weber says that husbands need to learn a foreign language—they must learn to "speak woman." Step #4 highlights that a man needs to learn to love his wife the way she wants to be loved.

 **Breaking the Ice** 15 MINUTES

LEADER: The first "Breaking the Ice" question lets couples tell more of their stories. The second invites discussion about family backgrounds. The third is a quick glance at ways to show love. Choose any or all of the questions that fit your group.

1. Briefly share what your first date was like with your spouse. What were your first impressions of your future mate?

2. When you were growing up, how did your father show love to your mother? How did his approach go over with your mother?
   - ○ Lots of hugging and kissing
   - ○ Flowers and gifts
   - ○ Occasional signs of affection
   - ○ Taking her places and spending time together
   - ○ Grunts and belches
   - ○ Helping her around the house
   - ○ Other: _____

3. If time, money, and talent weren't issues, what would you consider the best way for a man to express love to his wife?

- ○ Jewelry or other gifts
- ○ A cruise
- ○ A romantic getaway
- ○ Original poetry or music
- ○ Some serious passion
- ○ A day for her to pamper herself
- ○ Other: _____

LEADER: Encourage each person to share a key insight from "A Question to Take to Your Heart" or "Date Night". This should only take a couple of minutes each, but allow a little more time if someone has something inspiring to share. Affirm couples that had interesting experiences with serving one another.

4. How did the question for your heart regarding submission and the "Submit-to-Your-Spouse" adventure go? Can you share a key insight or memorable moment with the group?

Discovering the Truth 20-25 MINUTES

STEP #4 – Love Your Wife the Way She Wants to Be Loved

In Session Two, we discovered that men must love their wives with understanding and with intention. Today, we'll explore 10 practical ways to help make that love a reality for the special ladies in each of our homes. NOTE: Not one man will achieve God's ideal in all these areas, but he doesn't have to. Each husband should focus on his wife's particular needs and love languages, and then strive to love her more and better as time goes on.

LEADER: In each section of the 10 areas, ask some men in the group to read Bible passages and brief summaries before each set of questions.

NOTE: You will need to move along through each area to cover them all. Or, you may decide as a group to extend Session Four into two group sessions. Be sure to leave at least 15 minutes for the "Connecting" segment at the end of your time together.

(1) Tenderness

Therefore, God's chosen ones, holy and loved, put on heartfelt compassion, kindness, humility, gentleness, and patience.

COLOSSIANS 3:12

The first thing most women think of when they describe love is *tenderness*. They want to be treated gently, thoughtfully, and sensitively. They want to be talked to tenderly, touched tenderly, and listened to tenderly.

1a. As we look at some key elements of tenderness in Colossians 3:12, what behaviors can a husband practice to communicate loving tenderness to his wife?

1b. What are some barriers that prevent men from displaying heartfelt compassion and gentleness?

(2) Esteem and Appreciation

[10] Who can find a capable wife? She is far more precious than jewels. [11] The heart of her husband trusts in her, and he will not lack anything good. ... [25] Strength and honor are her clothing, ... [28] Her sons rise up and call her blessed. Her husband also praises her: [29] "Many women are capable, but you surpass them all!"

PROVERBS 31:10-11,25, 28-29

Most women associate love with *esteem* and *appreciation*. Most men treat women with high esteem during courtship. They tell women they're beautiful. They express admiration and devotion. Unfortunately, after marriage most husbands begin to take their wives for granted and do little to build their wives' self-esteem. Wives invest a lot of their time, energy, and the very essence of their lives in creating their homes and caring for their families. Women need to be built up through appreciation; often they receive very little unless it comes from their husbands.

a. The woman in Proverbs 31 is clearly honored and appreciated by her husband. In what ways have you seen men esteem their wives with words and actions?

b. What are some factors in our culture, lifestyles, and mindsets that can prevent men from showing honor and expressing appreciation to their wives?

3) Affection

You have captured my heart, my sister, my bride. You have captured my heart with one glance of your eyes, with one jewel of your necklace. ¹⁰ How delightful your love is, my sister, my bride. Your love is much better than wine, and the fragrance of your perfume than any balsam.

SONG OF SONGS 4:9-10

Love to most women means *affection*. However affectionate behavior isn't defined as foreplay before sexual intercourse. Some women can find themselves trapped between desiring physical contact and dreading it because their husbands always view hugs and kisses as come-ons for sex. Men need to learn to be forthright in showing affection for their wives as the husband in the Song of Songs does—speaking romantically and intimately, holding and caressing them in non-sexual ways.

3a. The answers may be different for each woman in the group, but what are some practical ways husbands demonstrate for their wives that their hearts are captured?

3b. What obstacles do husbands and wives need to overcome to enhance affection and romance in marriage?

(4) Help

[Jesus, referring to Himself said:] "For even the Son of Man did not come to be served, but to serve, and to give His life—a ransom for many."

MARK 10:45

Many women feel loved when their husbands gladly give them *help*. Wives appreciate home repairs and home-improvement projects, but they feel loved by husbands who willingly help with chores such as vacuuming, bed making, laundry, and dishes. This kind of service is both a way of assisting and of expressing appreciation. It is one practical way to esteem your wife.

4a. Jesus set the model for serving others. What household chores could husbands do that would genuinely help as well as communicate love to their wives?

4b. In what ways do husbands struggle with helping out around the house?

(5) Listening

My dearly loved brothers, understand this: everyone must be quick to hear, slow to speak, and slow to anger.

JAMES 1:19

Listening communicates love to many women. Wives want their husbands' full attention when they talk. After a day at the office or a day at home with preschoolers, wives long for eye contact and expressions of understanding. They don't need to hear what they should have done differently to fix everything. They want to be heard and to be taken seriously.

5. What are some barriers that prevent men from being good listeners—"quick to hear, slow to speak, and slow to anger"? What behaviors let wives know that their husbands are truly listening?

(6) Provision

Now if anyone does not provide for his own relatives, and especially for his household, he has denied the faith and is worse than an unbeliever.

1 TIMOTHY 5:8

Wives typically connect their husbands' love with *provision*. God placed the burden of family support on the husband. Husbands who lie on the couch and watch sports all weekend without lifting a finger to help with the kids or the house don't communicate love to their wives. The Bible strongly condemns husbands who won't work to provide for their families.

(7) Protection and Security

[Jesus praying for his disciples said:] "While I was with them, I was protecting them by Your name that You have given Me. I guarded them and not one of them is lost, except the son of destruction [Judas], so that the Scripture may be fulfilled."

JOHN 17:12

Most women associate their husbands' love with a sense of *security*. Jesus again sets the model for protecting and guarding our loved ones; He took this responsibility very seriously. In addition to protecting their wives, husbands need to keep their wives at ease about how solid the foundations of their marriages are. A Christian counselor once said, "Women don't do well with fear. Having a lazy husband, an angry husband, an unpredictable husband, or a philandering husband destroys their security."

6. What are some behaviors you've observed from husbands that can fuel a sense of insecurity and fear in their wives?

7. What are some specific ways that men help their wives to feel safe—physically, emotionally, and spiritually? (Consider the 1 Timothy and John passages, as well as your life experiences.)

(8) Development

28 In the same way, husbands should love their wives as their own bodies. He who loves his wife loves himself. 29 For no one ever hates his own flesh, but provides and cares for it, just as Christ does for the church.

EPHESIANS 5:28-29

Loving husbands are devoted to their wives' *development*. This is part of loving their wives as Christ loves the church. The word "husband" comes from a word that means "house provider" or "house manager." Husbands need to study their wives spiritually, physically, and intellectually and stimulate their growth.

8. Women: In what areas would you most appreciate your husband's assistance in developing yourself during this season of your married life?

9. Men: In what specific ways could you see yourself stimulating or providing for your wife to grow and develop in an area of her interest or expertise?

(9) Sexual Fulfillment

[3] A husband should fulfill his marital duty to his wife, and likewise a wife to her husband. [4] A wife does not have authority over her own body, but her husband does. Equally, a husband does not have authority over his own body, but his wife does. [5] Do not deprive one another—except when you agree, for a time, to devote yourselves to prayer. Then come together again; otherwise, Satan may tempt you because of your lack of self-control.

1 CORINTHIANS 7:3-5

Most women hope love will provide them with *sexual fulfillment*. While it's true that in many married couples the man wants sexual relations more often than the woman, that isn't always the case. Husbands need to understand the sexual desires of their wives and respect them. They should make it their goal to learn to delight their wives physically, rather than pursuing sexual activity primarily to satisfy themselves. This will require discussions with their wives about what sexual activities give them pleasure and which ones don't.

You will discuss the sexual aspect of your marriage as the focus of your "Date Night" this week.

(10) Quality Time

[1] There is an occasion for everything, and a time for every activity under heaven: ... [4] a time to weep and a time to laugh; a time to mourn and a time to dance.

ECCLESIASTES 3:1,4

The Book of Ecclesiastes points out that time is a precious commodity and that there is a time for everything that is set as a priority in life. Many women love for their husbands to spend *quality time* with them. Marriage counselors often advocate a regular date night to provide a setting for focused time between wives and husbands. Whether it's a date night or a commitment to put down the newspaper and turn off the television to engage in meaningful conversation with each other, husbands must find ways to devote time to relating with their wives. Their time will be well invested.

You will discuss this area of quality time during the "Connecting" time.

 # Embracing the Truth 10-15 MINUTES

Making STEP #4 Work

LEADER: This next activity gives each couple a private opportunity for affirmation and discussion. Be sure each couple knows what to do. Help them spread out through your meeting area to achieve adequate privacy. Bring everyone together after 10 minutes for "Connecting".

Find a quiet corner where you can talk just with your spouse about these next two questions. If your spouse did not attend, spend some time by yourself thinking through this question; then discuss it with him or her at home.

0. Wife: Which of these 10 expressions of love do you value most? Why? In which one does your husband score the highest? Which one would benefit your marriage most if your husband practiced it more?

1. Men: Which of these "supportive" expressions of love do you find hardest to practice? Why? After hearing your wife's specific love needs, what one or two things can you commit to doing to enhance your marriage?

Connecting 15 MINUTES

Most, if not all, of the 10 ways husbands can love their wives as outlined in this session depend on men carving out time in their schedules to devote to cherishing, providing for, and nurturing their wives. The idea of a date night for married couples grows out of the need to create a mechanism that helps husbands and wives regularly come together in settings that encourage conversation in relaxed, if not romantic, settings.

1. What activities do you and your spouse enjoy doing together?

2. Which one of these activities results in the most conversation? How often do you do this?

3. Get together with another couple. Talk about how each of you can implement a regular date night into your weekly routine. Discuss how each couple will hold the other accountable for having a weekly date night through the balance of this study and beyond.

While still in your sub-groups, spend time praying for each person as he or she strive to develop a greater sense of love and intimacy in marriage.

Share any prayer requests with the entire group and record them in the space below. Remember to pray regularly for them between now and the next session.

Prayer Requests:

 # Taking it Home

LEADER: "Taking it Home" this week provides "A Question to Take to God" and a discussion-oriented couple's activity. Encourage everyone to complete both projects before the next session.

When couples date, most of them talk a lot about everything. For some reason, those same couples, after they get married, assume they don't need to talk much anymore. They think they should just know what each another wants and how each other wants and how each other feels about things. Not surprisingly, they end up in misunderstandings. Men who want to value, guard, and nurture their wives need to sharpen their communication skills.

Before the next small-group session, talk with God and with your mate about aspects of how you communicate within your marriage. Complete the following:

(1) A Question to Take to God on page 60

(2) A Date Night on page 61

LEADER: Have each couple set a date, time, and location for the "Date Night" … right now before you close your session. This conversation about sex may be the most sensitive couple's assignment of the study. Encourage couples to choose a time when they will have unhurried privacy.

When? _____ Where? _____

SNEAK PEEK
Next time we meet, we'll look at 7 practical ways wives can show love and respect to their husbands. Wives, don't miss this!

A QUESTION TO TAKE TO GOD

Ask God for the guidance you need to make changes in your life. Don't expect God to answer with some fancy theological language. He tends to be amazingly practical. Talk to God, and then wait on Him until He responds. Be sure to write down what you hear from Him.

The spirit of a man is the lamp of the LORD, searching all the innermost parts of his being.
Proverbs 20:27 (NASB)

✚ Is communication and connection with my wife or husband a area that I am weak in or need to improve? Jesus, please speak into this area of my life and bring healing, so I can love the way You do. Take us to deeper levels of communication as a couple.

DATE NIGHT

Most of us don't talk much about our sex lives. We tend to engage in sexual activity in a hit-or-miss fashion with little feedback about whether we are pleasing our mates. Before the next session, carve out at least an hour of time to sit down and talk about sex. Choose a time when you are both rested and not rushed.

This probably won't be an easy conversation to have. Don't argue or be defensive if you discover an area of disagreement. Make it your goal to learn what your mate thinks about an aspect of your marriage that you may not have talked much about.

✠ Men ask your wife to tell you what sexual practices she enjoys. Ask her what lovemaking makes her feel cherished. Ask her if there are any sexual activities that make her feel uncomfortable.

✠ Women ask your husband to tell you what sexual practices he enjoys. Ask him what responses on your part mean a lot to him. Ask him what he wants to express to you through lovemaking.

At the end of this conversation, embrace or hold hands and individually thank God for your mate's willingness to talk with you about such an intimate topic. Ask for wisdom to understand and act on what you heard.

SCRIPTURE NOTES

PROVERBS 31:10-11,25, 28-29

31:10-31 In its original language this passage was an acrostic poem. Each line began with the next letter of the Hebrew alphabet.

31:25 laugh. She is prepared for the future because strength and honor are what she is clothed in. The value placed on her by her husband no doubt encourages her to press on.

31:29 capable. This woman enjoys a good reputation not only in the community but also in her own household where her weaknesses would be most evident. She is deserving of praise and her husband and children recognize this and appreciate her.

ECCLESIASTES 3:1,4

3:1-22 time. The teacher proves that humans are unable to alter God's sovereign plan. He first gives the human view of time (vv. 1-8), then God's view of time (vv. 9-22). The lesson here is that we should learn to view life by God's perception of time (*kairos*) instead of by our watches (*chronos*). Only God knows the best timing for human history; therefore, we must trust God's timing rather than our own perceptions. Time is a precious commodity and there is a time for everything that is set as a priority in life.

SONG OF SONGS 4:9-10

4:9 captured my heart, my sister. In love poetry of the ancient Near East, lovers often call each other "brother" and "sister" (vv. 10,12; 5:1) as terms of endearment. Men should be forthright in showing affection for their wives as the husband in this song does—to speak romantically and intimately, to hold and caress them in non-sexual ways, to show their wives that their hearts have been "captured."

MARK 10:45

10:45 ransom. In the first century, a slave or a prisoner could gain freedom if a purchase price (ransom) was paid. Jesus would pay the ransom price "for many" by His death (Titus 2:14; 1 Peter 1:18-19). In the same way, we need to give ourselves in service to our spouses.

JOHN 17:12

17:12 protecting them. Jesus again sets the model, this time for protecting and guarding our loved ones; He took this responsibility very seriously. In addition to protecting their wives, husbands need to keep their wives at ease about how solid the foundations of their marriages are.

1 CORINTHIANS 7:3-5

7:3 fulfill his marital duty. While it's true that in the experience of many married couples the man wants sexual relations more often than the woman, that isn't always the case. Husbands need to understand the sexual desires of their wives and respect them. They should make it their goal to learn to delight their wives physically rather than pursuing sexual activity primarily to satisfy themselves

7:5 deprive. Literally, "rob." For one partner to opt out of sexual relations under the guise of spirituality is a form of robbery. Abstinence is allowed under two conditions: both partners agree, and it is for a limited time. *prayer.* The purpose of such abstinence is prayer. *lack of self-control.* Paul assumes that a couple would not be married in the first place if they did not feel any sexual desire, and thus they ought to fulfill such desires legitimately, lest they be tempted to fall into adultery.

EPHESIANS 5:28-29

:28 their own bodies. Eve was Adam's flesh and bones—she came from his body. Believers in Christ are His body. When a man and a woman marry, they become "one flesh" (Gen. 2:24; Eph. 5:31). The man's deep-rooted instinct to care for himself should carry over to caring for her.

COLOSSIANS 3:12

:12-17 put on. Paul uses the image of putting on new clothes to show how true spirituality involves "wearing" the Christ-like qualities of love, peace, and thankfulness (Rom. 3:14). *heartfelt compassion.* The first thing most women think of when they describe love is tenderness. They want to be treated gently, thoughtfully, and sensitively. They want to be talked to tenderly, touched tenderly, listened to tenderly.

JAMES 1:19

19 slow to speak. One needs to consider carefully what is to be said, rather than impulsively and carelessly launching into unwise words. *slow to anger.* James does not forbid anger. He does caution against responding in anger at every opportunity.

Speaking Your Husband's Love Language

HOW TO SUCCEED IN LOVING YOUR HUSBAND

In our last session we studied Step #4, *Love Your Wife the Way She Wants to Be Loved*, and examined 10 qualities husbands need to work at in order to love their wives. The primary command God gives husbands in the New Testament is to love their wives (Ephesians 5:25). God clearly thinks it's an extremely manly thing to do.

This week, we will study seven ways that a wife can best show love and respect to her husband. Step #5 in creating an amazing marriage highlights the importance of a woman learning to love her husband so that he feels her respect and confidence.

 # Breaking the Ice   15 MINUTES

LEADER: The first "Breaking the Ice" question is just for grins. The second lets group members express some positive and negative emotions about the realities of love. The third lets couples tell more of their stories. Choose any or all of them that will benefit your group.

1. Which of these television wives have you most enjoyed watching? Why?
   - ○ Annie Camden from *7th Heaven*
   - ○ Laura Petrie from *The Dick Van Dyke Show*
   - ○ Louise Jefferson from *The Jeffersons*
   - ○ Edith Bunker from *All in the Family*
   - ○ Jill Taylor from *Home Improvements*
   - ○ Other: _____

2. Which movie title best captures the way love plays out in your marriage on a bad day? How about a good day? Why?
   - ○ *Life Is Beautiful*
   - ○ *The Bride of Frankenstein* or *Revenge of the Mummy*
   - ○ *A Walk to Remember*
   - ○ *One Flew Over the Cuckoo's Nest*
   - ○ *As Good As It Gets*
   - ○ *To Hell and Back*
   - ○ *Some Like It Hot*
   - ○ Other: _____

As newlyweds, when did you begin to realize you and your mate had different ideas about how to express love or be romantic? In what ways have you come closer together in your understanding?

. Take a little time for some very general sharing regarding your conversations about sex. How hard were those conversations to have? What did you learn about talking together about sensitive and intimate topics?

 # Discovering the Truth 20-25 MINUTES

In Session Three, we discovered that women must become "courageous completers" along with respecting their husbands. Wives play a vital role in the success of their husbands and their lives together. Today, we'll explore ways you can love and build up your husband by honoring him, supporting/helping him, and pleasing him.

STEP #5 – Love Your Husband By Giving Him Your Respect and Confidence

And He said to Adam ... The ground is cursed because of you. You will eat from it by means of painful labor all the days of your life. ... ¹⁸ It will produce thorns and thistles for you ... You will eat bread by the sweat of your brow until you return to the ground.

GENESIS 3:17-19

¹⁰ Who can find a capable wife? She is far more precious than jewels. ¹¹ The heart of her husband trusts in her, and he will not lack anything good. ¹² She rewards him with good, not evil, all the days of her life.

PROVERBS 31:10-1

A capable wife is her husband's crown, but a wife who causes shame is like rottenness in his bones.

PROVERBS 12:

Honor Him

1. The curse Adam brought on all men included "painful labor," "thorns and thistles," and "sweat" (Genesis 3:17-19). What are some different ways you have seen this curse demonstrated in your work life (men) or in your husband's work life (women)? How can wives encourage and *appreciate* their husbands as they strive to provide for their families in this difficult and frustrating world?

2. Men spend a lot of time in hostile workplace environments and they want to know that at home their wives *respect* them. What are some ways that wives can "reward him with good" (Proverbs 31:12) in order to build their husbands up? What words or actions "reward him with ... evil" or damage him emotionally and spiritually?

3. *Honor* is important to men. Most husbands expect to look better as their wives handle situations graciously. How can a woman be her "husband's crown"? (See Proverbs 12:4 and 31:10-12). What are some ways she can bring "rottenness to his bones"?

     The first quality most men identify when they think of a loving wife is *respect*. Women, treat your husbands respectfully in the privacy of your homes, even when you are disagreeing. Treat them respectfully when you talk about them to others. Resist doing or saying things that will cut the emotional legs out from under them.

     The second quality many men link to loving them is *appreciation*. Men work in a rat race where rats win. Husbands need to know their wives appreciate their efforts to provide and care for their families. NOTE: Envy can be an enemy of appreciation. Not all husbands are well-paid executives. Be careful of unfair comparisons.

     The third quality many men connect to a loving wife is *honor*. Most wives realize that their husbands' sense of identity is enhanced by their wives. Men swell with pride when their wives receive recognition. On the other hand, nothing dishonors a husband more than a wife whose character brings reproach on his home.

Support Him

Throughout this study, we have discussed a variety of ways a wife "completes" and "helps" her husband. The two qualities in this section have to do with home-related matters.

Therefore, I want younger women to marry, have children, manage their households, and give the adversary no opportunity to accuse us.

1 TIMOTHY 5:14

She rises while it is still night and provides food for her household and portions for her servants. ... ²¹ She not afraid for her household when it snows, for all in her household are doubly clothed. ... ²⁷ She watches over the activities of her household and is never idle.

PROVERBS 31:15,21,27

. Paul encouraged women to learn how to "manage their households" (1 Timothy 5:14). This in no way implies that husbands don't need to share in housework. It means that generally wives accept the responsibility for a well-ordered home. In what specific ways should wives be *home managers*?

. Beyond the obvious home décor and cleanliness, how can wives make their homes places of order, righteousness, peace, and love—havens of love and security in the midst of a harsh world?

. Proverbs 31 discusses some ways a wife should have a *family focus*. If children enter the picture, wives become mothers. Although fathers must accept their responsibilities in child rearing, mothers typically play the primary hands-on role of nurturer within their families. What are some ways that you have observed "stay at home" and "working" women "watch over the activities of her household"?

. How do you think wives and husbands should share in home management and child-rearing? How do responsibilities shift when both husbands and wives work outside the home?

The fourth quality, most husbands need from a loving wife is *home management*. Husbands need a haven of love and security in the midst of a harsh world. Most husbands think of *family focus* as a fifth quality associated with a loving wife. Overall it could be said of her, "She looks well to the ways of her household" (Proverbs 31:27, NASB). Even if a woman works in a business, her heart must still be strongly tied to her home and family.

Please Him

Be careful not to misconstrue the two qualities discussed in this section as sexist ramblings. Men tend to be visually stimulated and interested in sexual activity. Those are facts to take into account, not diseases to cure.

³ Your adornment must not be merely external—braiding the hair, and wearing gold jewelry, or putting on dresses; ⁴ but let it be the hidden person of the heart, with the imperishable quality of a gentle and quiet spirit, which is precious in the sight of God.

1 PETER 3:3-4 (NASB)

She makes her own bed coverings; her clothing is fine linen and purple.

PROVERBS 31:2

¹⁸ Let your fountain be blessed, and take pleasure in the wife of your youth. ¹⁹ A loving doe, a graceful fawn— let her breasts always satisfy you; be lost in her love forever.

PROVERBS 5:18-1

³ A husband should fulfill his marital duty to his wife, and likewise a wife to her husband. ⁴ A wife does not have authority over her own body, but her husband does. Equally, a husband does not have authority over his own body, but his wife does. ⁵ Do not deprive one another—except when you agree, for a time, to devote yourselves to prayer. Then come together again; otherwise, Satan may tempt you because of your lack of self-control.

1 CORINTHIANS 7:3-

8. The men in this group married the women in this group because they found them *attractive*. A combination of physical, emotional, and personal traits about each woman appealed to her man. What picture does 1 Peter 3:3-4 paint of attractiveness as compared to our culture's obsession with youth and beauty? Considering the passages in 1 Peter and Proverbs, as well as your own experiences, how can wives continue to make themselves more attractive to their husbands?

. *Sexual fulfillment* is not the same thing as frequent sex. Most husbands find true sexual fulfillment in the responsiveness of their wives. How does our attitude and approach to sexual intimacy change when we focus more on pleasing our mates than on pleasing ourselves (1 Corinthians 7:3-5) and on taking pleasure in each other (Proverbs 5:18)?

We've seen that the sixth quality men tend to look for in a loving wife is *attractiveness*. Attractiveness truly does apply to a woman's inner qualities. Although a wife should strive to look her best, the physical dimension will deteriorate over time. But as that occurs, the inner dimensions can become even more appealing.

Men also desire *sexual fulfillment* from their relationships with their wives. Good sex for men is sex that their wives enjoy. Obviously, there will be times when one partner greatly enjoys a sexual contact and the other doesn't as much. However, mutual delight is an important goal for couples to discuss and pursue. 1 Corinthians 7:5 is not a "club" to use on a disinterested mate. It's a warning about the spiritual dangers of sexual dysfunction. As a couple grows closer over the years, their love should deepen and be fully satisfying.

 # Embracing the Truth   10-15 MINUTES

Making STEP #5 Work

Find a quiet corner where you can talk just with your spouse about these next two questions. If your spouse did not attend, spend some time by yourself thinking through this question; then discuss this topic with him or her at home.

10. Men: Which of these seven expressions of love do you value most? Why? In which one does your wife score the highest? Which one would benefit your marriage most if your wife practiced it more?

11. Women: Which of these "honor/appreciate," "support," or "pleasing" expressions of love do you find hardest to practice? Why? After hearing your husband's specific love needs, what one or two things can you commit to doing to enhance your marriage?

 **Connecting** 15 MINUTES

The seven aspects of being loving wives discussed in this session will work themselves out uniquely in each marriage. Use this community-building time to affirm your commitment to one another as a couple.

LEADER: Use this "Connecting" time to develop a sense of community in your group, as you continue to grow closer and build one another up. Encourage everyone to join in and to be open with one another Address Question 1 to the women and Question 2 to the men. For Question 3, take turns, as everyone in the group participates.

1. Women: What new insights have you gained about loving and respecting your husband? Do you plan to implement any changes based on these insights?

2. Men: What new insights have you gained in the last two sessions about your responsibility to love and lead your wife? Do you plan to implement any changes based on these insights?

3. First, each *husband* should tell his wife something about her he is proud of, and then one thing he appreciates about how she honors, supports, or pleases him. Second, each *wife* should tell her husband something about him she is proud of, and then one thing she appreciates about how he cherishes, provides for, or nurtures her.

Share group prayer requests and record them in the space below. Pray together now for any changes couples are trying to make to enhance their love relationships.

Prayer Requests:

Taking it Home

When men hear about being loving leaders, they may think they are noble and exalted. When women hear about being courageous completers or helpers, they may feel as though they've been demoted. However, a woman also has an exalted role in marriage: she has a nurturing ministry, and she reflects God's nurturing side. Through her contribution, she brings God's help to bear on her husband and family. "A Question to Take to Your Heart" encourages both wives and husbands to consider how conducive the climate of their marriage is for the love and intimacy God intends.

(1)   A Question to Take to Your Heart on page 72

(2)   A Date Night on page 73

When? _____ Where? _____

SNEAK PEEK

Next time we meet, we'll look at how a classic New Testament couple modeled God's design specifications for marriage.

A Question to Take to Your Heart

Once again, look into your heart and mind to consider the sometimes hidden factors that motivate your thoughts and actions. What do you really feel God is like? Does He seem to get very involved in your life? What fears and insecurities haunt you? What unfulfilled dreams feed your fantasies? What gives you joy and real delight? Be sure to write down your insights to help you act on them.

WOMEN: What within my heart helps me to love and respect my husband the way I do?

What prevents me from being a more loving and respectful wife to my husband?

MEN: What within my heart helps me to love and cherish my wife the way I do?

What prevents me from being a more loving and adoring husband to my wife?

DATE NIGHT

Last week your "Date Night" consisted of a heavy conversation about your sex life. This week minimize the talking and the seriousness. Give your mate non-sexual physical pleasure. You know what he or she likes. You should each choose and initiate a back rub, a foot massage, a long soak in the tub, etc.

Wives, take the initiative to put this "Date Night" on the calendar. When the agreed-upon day arrives, serve your husbands first. Then husbands, it's your turn to serve your wives. Directed conversation is not required. Just enjoy each other's company with no particular agenda. If you like, share some your dreams for the future—this is another component to an amazing marriage.

To close your "Date Night", hold hands and pray for each other about the success of your plans and dreams for the future.

SCRIPTURE NOTES

GENESIS 3:17-19

3:18 you will eat from it by means of painful labor. As part of the curse for his sin, there would be a price to be paid for the good things in life. Adam was still able to grow food and feed himself and his family. But now that task meant painful and difficult labor. His dominion over the earth would be a struggle that would end in death.

3:19 ground. Referring to death. Adam's life and sustenance came from the ground. In his death, he would return to that same state. Until the day he died, providing for himself and his family would require difficult and painful labor.

PROVERBS 5:18-19; 12:4; 31:10-12, 15, 21-22 27

5:18 take pleasure in the wife of your youth. Even as a married couple grows older, they should be enjoying physical and sexual pleasures together. This is a picture of long-term committed love in action. As a couple grows closer over the years, their love should deepen and be fully satisfying.

12:4 her husband's crown. Because she is capable, she elevates her husband and is an invaluable asset to him (see also Proverbs 31:10).

31:10-31 In its original language this passage was an acrostic poem. Each line began with the next letter of the Hebrew alphabet.

31:10 more precious than jewels. This refers to the value of a capable wife to her husband. Proverbs 12:4 says that she is her "husband's crown." Because she is capable and respects her husband, he can trust in her. This security is a priceless gift.

31:12 rewards him with good. Most wives realize that their husbands' sense of identity is enhanced by their wives. Men swell with pride when their wives receive recognition. On the other hand, nothing dishonors a husband more than a wife whose character brings reproach on his home. A capable wife respects her husband

31:15 rises while it is still night. This woman is the opposite of the slacker who loves to sleep (6:9; 20:13). Her heart is focused on the needs of her family, and she takes care of them as well as her household.

31:22 fine linen and purple. She makes herself attractive. Her own clothes reflect her family's strong position. Purple, made from a rare dye from shellfish, was a color for royalty.

1 CORINTHIANS 7:3-5

7:3 marital duty ... a wife to her husband. With many married couples, the man wants sexual relations more often than the woman; this is a need to understand for the wife rather than a problem to be fixed. Wives need to understand the sexual desires of their husbands and respect them. However, mutual delight is an important goal for couples to discuss and pursue.

7:5 deprive. Literally, "rob." For one partner to opt out of sexual relations under the guise of spirituality is a form of robbery. However, this verse is not a "club" to use on a disinterested mate. It's a warning about the spiritual dangers of sexual dysfunction. It is also a challenge for women to learn how to respond to their husbands, and for men to learn how to show tender physical affection to their wives. Abstinence is allowed under two conditions: both partners agree, and it is for a limited time. *prayer.* The purpose of such abstinence is prayer. *lack of self-control.* Paul assumes that a couple would not be married in the first place if they did not feel any sexual desire, and thus they ought to fulfill

such desires legitimately, lest they be tempted
to fall into adultery.

I TIMOTHY 5:14

5:14 manage their households. This in no way
implies that husbands don't need to share
in housework. It means that generally a wife
accepts the responsibility for a well-ordered
home. Her home should be a haven of love
and security in the midst of a harsh world.
no opportunity to accuse. In this context, the
younger widows' behavior had become the
grounds on which others were speaking
evil of the church. Paul continues with
his concern that the church not be judged
negatively by the surrounding culture.

I PETER 3:3-4

3:3 not merely external. Attractiveness is not only
a synonym for physical beauty. Attractiveness
truly does apply to a woman's inner qualities.
Although a wife should strive to look her
best, the physical dimension will deteriorate
over time. But as that occurs, the inner
dimensions of attractiveness can become
even more appealing. This verse obviously
does not prohibit jewelry, hairstyles, or
clothes.

A Couple Worth Modeling

THE "EAGLE" AND THE "WISE WOMAN"

Last week in Step #5, *Love Your Husband By Giving Him Your Respect and Confidence*, we explored seven ways that a wife can best show love and respect for her husband. Our study highlighted that a woman needs to learn to love her husband so that he feels her respect and confidence. She can best express her love by respecting him, supporting him, and pleasing him.

In this final session, we'll consider the classic, biblical example of Priscilla and Aquila. The name Aquila mean, "Eagle," and Priscilla means something like "Wise Woman." Aquila was a husband who led while loving; Priscilla was a wife who flourished while following his lead. They model seven qualities for which married couples should strive.

 # Breaking the Ice   15 MINUTES

LEADER: The first two "Breaking the Ice" questions encourage husbands and wives to assess how they are alike and different. The third addresses some basic assumptions about marital success.

1. Which of these animals best describes you? Why?

   ○ The busy otter
   ○ The slow, but certain tortoise
   ○ The wise owl
   ○ The courageous lion
   ○ The trusty Labrador retriever
   ○ Other: _____

2. Which of the animals in Question 1 would you have picked for your mate? If your choice differs from his or hers, what prompted you to pick it?

. When you envision the ideal married couple, which one of these characteristics stands out the most for you? Why?

- ○ Happiness
- ○ Unity of purpose
- ○ Security
- ○ Devotion to one another
- ○ Passion
- ○ Other: _____

4. How did your question for your heart about loving—cherishing or respecting—your spouse go? Can you share a key insight? How did you enjoy doing something for your mate to give him or her pleasure? What keeps us from doing things like that more often?

Discovering the Truth 20-25 MINUTES

There aren't many married couples described in any detail in the New Testament. We don't know much about Elizabeth and Zechariah or Mary and Joseph except what happened concerning the birth of their famous sons. Peter must have been married; he had a mother-in-law. Ananias and Sapphira illustrated what not to do. Pilate and King Agrippa had wives, but they played minor roles. However, there is one married couple that pops up four times in the New Testament. From these brief snatches of information an intriguing picture emerges of a classic couple.

STEP #6 – Your Marriage Is Unique; Let God Reveal Its Special Qualities

[Luke wrote:] [1] After this, [Paul] left from Athens and went to Corinth, [2] where he found a Jewish man named Aquila, a native of Pontus, who had recently come from Italy with his wife Priscilla because Claudius had ordered all the Jews to leave Rome. Paul came to them, [3] and being of the same occupation, stayed with them and worked, for they were tentmakers by trade. [4] He reasoned in the synagogue every Sabbath and tried to persuade both Jews and Greeks.

ACTS 18:1-4

[Paul wrote:] The churches of the Asian province greet you. Aquila and Priscilla greet you heartily in the Lord ...

1 CORINTHIANS 16:19

[Luke wrote:] So Paul, having stayed on for many days, said good-bye to the brothers and sailed away to Syria. Priscilla and Aquila were with him.

ACTS 18:18

[Paul wrote:] Give my greetings to Prisca and Aquila, my co-workers in Christ Jesus.

ROMANS 16:3

[Paul wrote:] Greet Prisca and Aquila.

2 TIMOTHY 4:19

LEADER: Discuss as many of these questions as time permits. The strongest application questions appear in the "Embracing the Truth" section. It will help to highlight in advance the questions you don't want to miss.

1. When we first meet this couple, they are referred to as "Aquila ... with his wife Priscilla" (Acts 18:2). Husband's names were traditionally given first in recognition of their leadership role in the home. Aquila's name is also first in 1 Corinthians 16:19 when Paul speaks in an official capacity. Why do you suppose then that Paul and Luke mention Priscilla (nickname Prisca) first in other personal references?

2. It is apparent from other passages later in this session that Priscilla is the more outgoing and outspoken person in this marriage. How might the strong and prominent personality of a wife affect the dynamics of the marriage relationship?

Aquila was the leader in his marriage, but he must have been a loving leader because Luke and Paul both unconventionally place Priscilla's name first. Aquila encouraged his wife to develop her gifts and flourish publicly. He demonstrated that men can lead without squelching their gifted wives. That's precisely the goal Christ has as He leads His church.

On her part, Priscilla was not seen by Paul, who clearly taught the God-given leadership role of the husband, as usurping her husband's role. The Apostle Paul, Luke, and the church did not feel any discomfort with Aquila's leadership in his marriage. The first quality of this classic couple is that they serve as *role models*: a husband who leads but loves, and a wife who is active and growing, yet respects and submits.

Eager to Learn and Serve

After this, [Paul] left from Athens and went to Corinth, ² where he found a Jewish man named Aquila ... with his wife Priscilla ... Paul came to them, ³ and being of the same occupation, stayed with them and worked, for they were tentmakers by trade. ⁴ He reasoned in the synagogue every Sabbath and tried to persuade both Jews and Greeks.

ACTS 18:1-4

¹⁸ So Paul, having stayed on for many days, said good-bye to the brothers and sailed away to Syria. Priscilla and Aquila were with him. ... ¹⁹ When they reached Ephesus he left them there, but he himself entered the synagogue and engaged in discussion with the Jews. ²⁰ And though they asked him to stay for a longer time, he declined, ²¹ but said good-bye and stated, "I'll come back to you again, if God wills." Then he set sail from Ephesus.

ACTS 18:18-21

¹⁹ The churches of the Asian province greet you. Aquila and Priscilla greet you heartily in the Lord, along with the church that meets in their home.

1 CORINTHIANS 16:19

3. For an extended period, this couple lived and worked with the Apostle Paul (Acts 18:3-4). What progression do you see in the passages above regarding Aquila's and Priscilla's spiritual knowledge and development?

4. How did all of the studying this couple did with Paul while he stayed in their home influence their lives and work for the Lord?

5. Priscilla and Aquila moved on with Paul from Corinth to Ephesus (Acts 18:18). After a time, they hosted the Ephesian church in their own home (1 Corinthians 16:19). What must it have been like to move to a big, hostile city like Ephesus in order to help plant a church, largely on their own? What resources and character qualities do you suppose it took for this couple to take on that challenge?

The second quality of this classic couple is that they show us how to be eager *students of God's truth*. They loved God and served their neighbors. Their lives were never the same after their intense encounter with Paul. If we want good marriages, we must study the Bible and spend time with God in prayer. We can learn all the principles of good marriages and have all kinds of good intentions, but only the Spirit of God using the Word of God can transform and empower us in our marriages.

Third they were *active disciples*, relocating their residence and business to reach out to others. Later they moved back to Rome (Rom. 16:3-5) before returning to Ephesus (2 Tim. 4:19). All the time they were actively serving God and people.

Our classic couple was *available* to God—the fourth quality they model for us. We need reminders of the temporary nature of where we are and what we do. Marriage ties us down with responsibility. If we're not careful, we can lose our edge for spiritual adventure. Aquila and Priscilla remind us that this world is not our home; our final destination is the kingdom of heaven as we serve that kingdom here.

Difference-Makers Through Relationships

[24] *A Jew named Apollos, a native Alexandrian, an eloquent man who was powerful in the Scriptures, arrived in Ephesus.* [25] *This man had been instructed in the way of the Lord; and being fervent in spirit, he spoke and taught the things about Jesus accurately, although he knew only John's baptism.* [26] *He began to speak boldly in the synagogue. After Priscilla and Aquila heard him, they took him home and explained the way of God to him more accurately.* [27] *When he wanted to cross over to Achaia, the brothers wrote to the disciples urging them to welcome him. After he arrived, he greatly helped those who had believed through grace.*

ACTS 18: 24-27

6. When you read Acts 18:24-27, how do you see Priscilla and Aquila acting as difference-makers? What roles were they playing in the "big story" of God's grand plan to spread the good news of Jesus and redeem the lives of people everywhere?

Aquila and Priscilla were difference-makers in the lives of people. The fifth quality of this couple is that they were *mentors*. When Apollos showed up in Ephesus teaching an incomplete version of the gospel, Priscilla and Aquila invested time in this brilliant young orator until he was ready to go out on his own. In the same way, we should be willing to mentor those who aren't as far along the path as we are in faith or in marriage.

Passionately Committed

³ Give my greetings to Prisca and Aquila, my co-workers in Christ Jesus, ⁴ who risked their own necks for my life. Not only do I thank them, but also so do all the Gentile churches. ⁵ Greet also the church that meets in their home.

ROMANS 16:3-5

²³ During that time [in Ephesus where Aquila and Priscilla were church leaders] there was a major disturbance about the Way [a name given the Christian movement]. ... ²⁸ they were filled with rage ... ²⁹ So the city was filled with confusion; and they rushed all together into the amphitheater, dragging along Gaius and Aristarchus, Macedonians who were Paul's traveling companions. ³⁰ Though Paul wanted to go in before the people, the disciples did not let him.

ACTS 19:23,28-30

Greet Prisca and Aquila, and the household of Onesiphorus.

2 TIMOTHY 4:19

7. What risks do you see this couple taking in these and other passages that we have looked at?

8. Paul's greeting to Prisca and Aquila in 2 Timothy was much later in their lives, more than 15 years after the events of Acts 18. Onesiphorus probably had been martyred in Rome because he had tended to Paul (2 Timothy 1:16). Aquila and Priscilla had stepped in to take care of Onesiphorus' widow and children. What does this story reveal about this couple?

The sixth quality this classic couple models for us is *willingness to take risks*. They "risked their own necks for my [Paul's] life" (Rom. 16:4). Corinth was a rough place, but our classic couple welcomed Paul into their home. At Ephesus they had the church in their home even when the city rioted because of Christianity. This couple was always on the cutting edge. They never looked for the easy way.

Finally, Aquila and Priscilla *finished strong*. They didn't start winding down as they grew older. Surely, no one was surprised by that. That's the kind of people they were. At a time when they could have slacked off and looked to someone younger to step in and take over, they pressed on in commitment to each other and to God.

Embracing the Truth   10-15 MINUTES

Making STEP #6 Work

9. As you've studied Aquila and Priscilla, why do you think is it necessary to draw close to God, personally and as a couple, in order to draw close to one another in marriage? What would it take for you to commit to some daily time alone with God and His Word? How do you feel about regular—even daily—prayer together with your spouse?

10. How can involvement in ministry as a couple stimulate a marriage and stretch it? How can we keep a balance between putting down roots as a family and being available to serve God and be difference-makers?

11. Consider the uniquenesses and special qualities of your marriage. Share one of these with the group.

♥ Connecting 15 MINUTES

For several weeks the couples in this group have shared intimately about their marriages and their faith in Jesus. This final opportunity for community-building gives us a chance to look back over the life of this study and to look ahead to how we want to incorporate the things we have learned into our marriages.

1. Go around the group and take turns sharing favorite memories from your time together during this study.

2. Share what general or specific goals you have set for yourself in your marriage because of this group.

3. Stand together in a circle and read the following passage of Scripture in unison.

> [4] *Love is patient; love is kind.*
> *Love does not envy; is not boastful; is not conceited;* [5] *does not act improperly;*
> *is not selfish; is not provoked; does not keep a record of wrongs;*
> [6] *finds no joy in unrighteousness, but rejoices in the truth;*
> [7] *bears all things, believes all things, hopes all things, endures all things.*
> [8] *Love never ends. ...*
> [13] *Now these three remain: faith, hope, and love.*
> *But the greatest of these is love.*
>
> I CORINTHIANS 13:4-8A, 13

Record group prayer requests in the space below as each couple seeks to recommit to building an amazing marriage and finishing strong together.

Prayer Requests:

 # Taking it Home

You will not be sharing anything from this "Taking it Home" session with your small group. Take some time in the next few days to reflect alone and with your spouse about this study of Some Assembly Required.

(1)   A Question to Take to God on page 85

(2)   A Date Night on page 86

LEADER: Have each couple set a date, time, and location for the "Date Night" … right now before you close your session.

When? _____   Where? _____

A Question to Take to God

You've studied *Some Assembly Required*, and participated in a small-group experience. Now it's time to ask God what your next step is and then move out as He directs! Give the Spirit time to direct your spirit in the way He wants you to move. As always, be sure to write down what you hear from God.

✠ God, what pleases You about our marriage? What is unique and special about our marriage? Where do You want us to go from here?

DATE NIGHT

Go to your local greeting card shop and purchase a romantic card from the section of *blank* cards. Take it home, write on the left side one sentence describing what your spouse means to you and on the right side one sentence telling what your marriage means to you. Go out to dinner at a nice restaurant and exchange cards at the end of the meal.

Keep the card you receive from your mate in a private place where you can see it and refer to it often as reminder of the love you share.

In your car as you get ready to leave the restaurant, hold hands while you thank God for one another and the marriage He has given you. Ask His blessing on your future together.

SCRIPTURE NOTES

ACTS 18:1-4,18-21,24-27; 19:23,28-30

18:1 The next stop for Paul on his second missionary journey was Corinth, a prosperous seaport 50 miles from Athens.

18:2 *Aquila ... Priscilla.* Aquila mean "Eagle," and Priscilla mean something like "Wise Woman." This couple apparently converted in Rome prior to meeting Paul. They became important coworkers with him. *Claudius had ordered all the Jews to leave Rome.* Because of uprisings in the Jewish community at Rome due to the influence of a man named Chrestus, riots broke out among the Roman Jews between those who believed in Jesus as the Messiah and those who did not. To solve the problem, the emperor ordered all Jews to leave! While the expulsion was not strictly enforced, for a time the Jews were forbidden to meet, which led many to leave anyway.

18:18 *Priscilla and Aquila were with him.* It is significant that Priscilla's name is mentioned first, ahead of her husband (Rom. 16:3; 2 Tim. 4:19). This was hardly ever done, and may indicate that Priscilla was the natural leader of the two. Passages that introduce the couple formally or officially name Aquila first as the head of his household (Acts 18:2; 1 Cor. 16:19).

18:25 While Apollos was an earnest, articulate believer in Jesus, he had not received the whole story of the gospel. Just what he was lacking is unclear, but, as the story in 19:1-7 indicates, he may not have heard of the coming of the Spirit promised to those who are baptized in the name of Jesus.

19:23 *major disturbance.* The silversmith trade made a great deal of money through the manufacture and sale of models of the goddess Artemis. Artemis was a goddess who combined belief in the Roman virgin goddess Diana with an Asian fertility goddess. The center for her worship was in Ephesus.

The message of Christianity was spreading and threatening to unravel the worship of Artemis, as well as the lucrative business in making silver shrines (19:27-28).

ROMANS 16:3-5

16:5 *the church ... in their home.* During the first two centuries, there were no special church buildings, so Christians met in the homes of their members (1 Cor. 16:19; Col. 4:15; Philem. 2). The growth of these churches was overwhelming. Priscilla and Aquila, and the other church hosts, had to be wealthy owners of large homes who generously used their resources to advance God's kingdom. Priscilla and Aquila relocated frequently. Aquila was from Pontus in northern Asia Minor, but he first appeared in Acts moving from Rome to Corinth (Acts 18:2). He and Priscilla relocated to Ephesus and hosted the church there (1 Cor. 16:19). Romans 16:3-5 indicates they were back in Rome and hosting that church. By the end of Paul's life, they were living in Ephesus again (2 Tim. 4:19).

1 CORINTHIANS 16:19

the church ... in their house. From its inception the Ephesian church served as the focal point for outreach into Asia (Acts 19:10). It's impossible to know how much of a role in its success Aquila and Priscilla played, but Paul clearly considered them invaluable coworkers in spreading the gospel (Rom. 16:3).

2 TIMOTHY 4:19

the household of Onesiphorus. Onesiphorus had gone from Ephesus to Rome to care for Paul during his imprisonment (1:16). He had exerted himself unusually in Paul's behalf, and it appears he died or was executed. At the end of 2 Timothy, Paul connected the household of Onesiphorus with Priscilla and Aquila. It appears God's mercy was coming to this household through them.

LEADER'S NOTES

This section contains ideas for leaders about directions in which you might want to steer the discussion of "Discovering the Truth" and "Embracing the Truth" questions for each of the six sessions of *Some Assembly Required.*

General Notes:

1. Try to keep discussions from getting bogged down, but give priority to addressing any needs within your group through "spontaneous prayer" and group support. You can ask whether your group would prefer to shorten an important discussion or extend your study duration.
2. Encourage people to bring and use their own Bibles.
3. Should difficult marital issues surface during this study, be prepared with names of pastors and Christian marriage counselors that you can refer a couple to.
4. Consider meeting for an additional session as a group to watch and discuss a movie with a strong love story, e.g. *The Notebook, Shall We Dance, Shadowlands, The Ideal Husband, The Preacher's Wife, Random Harvest, Kate and Leopold,* etc.

Session 1: A Marriage Made in Heaven

1. When God said, "Let *us* make man in *our* image, in *our* likeness" He revealed the plurality of His nature. The Persons of the Trinity consulted among Themselves collaboratively in creation. The humanity God created was plural and diverse— one man and one woman who completed one another in relationship.

2. This question can have a wide variety of answers. A wife completes her husbands as Eve completed Adam. She fills a loneliness void no one else can. Two have become one, so she partners with him in every aspect of life. She supports him emotionally in his workplace struggles. She shares his successes and failures. If God gives them children, she bears and nurtures them.

3. Knowing our spouses bear the image of God should cause us to respect and value them more. We should treat them with dignity, if not a little awe. We should never despise, degrade, or abuse them.

4. "The husband is the head of the home" can be a culturally loaded statement very different from the biblical teaching on headship and loving leadership. Often it refers to the man "bringing home the bacon" and making the decisions, while the woman has no say at all. When group members identify where they first heard this saying, ask them what they thought it meant.

5. A man must be under the authority of Christ before he can exercise servant leadership in his marriage. Husbands who are not aligned with God will try to lead their wives according to their basic outlook on life—anything from passive indifference to aggressive abuse.

6. First Corinthians 11:3 parallels the headship of man over woman with the headship of the Father over the Son. Headship appears to be a role between equals in which one takes responsibility for loving leadership and the other willingly accepts that.

8. It's important that everyone responds to this question. The answer influences the applications to be discussed in questions 9 and 10 and in the "Taking it Home" activity.

9. It isn't necessary for everyone to respond out loud to this, but be sure to ask if everyone has an action step in mind before moving on.

Session 2: Follow the Leader

1. If a husband loves as Christ loves, his love will be sacrificial. It will care about his beloved more than about self. It will be a patient, gentle love. It will be a love that encourages the beloved to become a better person.

2. A husband who loves his wife as his own body will regard anything good for his wife as good for himself. What pleases her pleases him. What grieves her grieves him. What honors her honors him.

3. The phrases "own body" and "own flesh" (Eph. 5:228-29) parallel the phrase "bone of my bone, and flesh of my flesh" in Genesis 2:23. Loving our wives "as our own bodies" find its roots in the original creation of humanity. Husband and wife are mystically united in "one flesh."

4. This question is meant to get group members to express their views about this controversial statement. While it is true that "women are generally physically weaker," the most important truth is that "women accept a vulnerable position when they submit when they submit to men."

5. Some ideas: He should know her personal strengths and weaknesses; her spiritual gifts; her dreams and ambitions. He should know the things that make her feel loved, as well as her fears so he can protect her. He should listen closely and observe her each day to sense how to respond to her joys and sorrows.

6. Your group responses might include ones like these. A husband's character establishes a standard of integrity for the family. His character sounds a tone

of compassion and kindness that others will follow or react to. His interest in spiritual matters influences those who follow him.

8. Potential responses: A wife should encourage her husband to stay tightly connected to God. She should openly express her insights, expectations, and desires but follow his lead (unless he is leading her into sin).

9. Potential responses: A husband should be studying God's Word and seeking His will so he can share spiritual wisdom with his wife to help her (and them) make good life choices.

Session 3: R-E-S-P-E-C-T

1. Some inherent risks in submission: A woman may marry an abusive man who will hurt her. She may marry an irresponsible man who won't support her. She may marry a sensual man who makes improper sexual demands on her. She may marry a control-freak who stifles every independent thought, word, or action.

2. Most will say that, while wives' submissive spirits have similar qualities in all marriages, submission will express itself uniquely in each marriage. The submission of a quiet woman will look different from that of an outgoing one. A woman with leadership gifts will probably end up carrying out different tasks in her marriage than one who finds deep satisfaction in domestic duties.

3. You may get answers such as respecting her husband's leadership, yielding graciously to his decisions after giving input, and trusting God to protect her and bless her through his leadership.

4. Both men and women are image-bearers of God, of equal dignity and worth. The roles people play should have no affect on how they treat others.

5. A "suitable" helper is not a passive wife, but rather one who courageously stands by her husband, lending the type of help that her husband needs in the specific situation he is in.

6. First Peter 3:1-2 stresses the persuasive force inherent in the example set by a submissive wife. This question asks group members to consider the impact of such an example to various audiences that might witness it. Responses will be limited only by the group's imagination.

7. Older women are experienced in all aspects of marriage and family life. They know both the struggles and the joys younger women will face. Unexpected nuggets of insight may emerge when women in the group share what they've learned from older women.

8. In addition to finding hope in the Lord, women can network with and find encouragement from other Christian women who are on the same pilgrimage of faith in their marriages.

9. Loving leadership and respectful submission are so difficult in marriage due to self-protection. Made in the image of God, husbands and wives are intended to seek the good of one another. Since the fall, husbands and wives are afraid to seek one another's good because they hear the lie of the Devil who says, "You can't put the welfare of anyone ahead of your own. It isn't safe." Look at all the blaming that occurred in Genesis 3:12-13.

10. Wives may tend to manipulate their husbands so they can feel in control and safe without resorting to a full-scale battle of wills that they might not win. Men may tend to dominate so they will appear to be masterful and in control, while concealing personal doubts about their effectiveness.

11. The Holy Spirit needs to expose the particular expressions of sin that each of us protects ourselves with and replace them with the fruit of the Spirit, which is "love, joy, peace, patience, kindness, goodness, faith, gentleness, self-control" (Gal. 5:22-23). We need to welcome the Holy Spirit's involvement in our lives.

Session 4: Speaking Your Wife's Love Language

1. Tenderness is displaying gentleness and sensitivity toward one's wife in the course of helping her, listening to her, or approaching her for intimacy. Some barriers to tenderness include fear of appearing weak, fear of rejection, unresolved anger, lack of sacrificial love, etc.

2. All the ways to express esteem and appreciation require personal, emotional, and spiritual maturity on the part of husbands. Older men in the group may have wisdom to share with younger ones. Many men are never taught to show honor and appreciation, or they just forget the importance of expressing what's in their hearts.

3. Affection is shown by anything a husband does that expresses how he cherishes his wife: words, touch, eye contact, gifts, notes, formal dates, spontaneous displays of love, etc. Husbands may not understand what communicates love to their wives, or they may not understand the importance of making affection and romance a priority.

5. Potential barriers: impatience, preoccupation with other activities, tiredness, lack of genuine concern (heart issue), etc.

6. This question is intended to help identify what gives wives the greatest sense of insecurity and fear to help husbands be aware of these things.

7. A wife whose husband helps her feels safe because she isn't facing her responsibilities alone. A wife whose husband listens to her feels safe because she knows her opinions matter to him. A wife whose husband provides for her feels safe because her home and lifestyle are secure. A wife who feels secure doesn't need to fear that her husband is pursuing other women in reality or fantasy.

8. This question gives women opportunity to express some of their dreams and ambitions both to a supportive group and to their husbands.

9. This question gives men opportunity to respond supportively to their wives and to start imagining how to help them grow and develop.

Session Five: Speaking Your Husband's Love Language

1. Deadlines are difficult. Business relationships can be very hard. Pressures, unexpected issues, boredom, and failures, to name a few can make labor "painful." Ways to encourage and appreciate men can vary, so it might be insightful to ask each husband lifts him up.

2. Respect is shown in both words and actions. James 3:10 says, "Out of the same mouth come cursing and blessing." Words can be powerful.

3. This question could give men opportunity to affirm their wives. Both men and women should consider how the strengths and character of a wife gives honor to her husband.

5. Much of what it takes to make a home a haven of love and security is centered on making this a priority, as well as being sensitive to the needs of each family member.

6. The key point regardless of specifics and circumstances is that a wife makes her family and home a key priority ... her heart is at home.

7. Your group will answer this in various ways. Basically, each couple should hammer out its own way of sharing home management and child-rearing consistent with the responsibilities the Bible lays out for husbands and wives.

8. This question gives your group the chance to express what's wrong with cultural attitudes toward youth and beauty and to affirm biblical standards of inner beauty. If group members tend to take different positions, have them clarify their ideas to one another.

9. This discussion could go many directions. Much of it will boil down to giving versus taking. Self-pleasing sexual activity is a *taking* behavior that uses the other partner. Other-pleasing sexual activity is a *giving* behavior that serves the other partner.

Session Six: A Couple Worth Modeling

2. They appear to be a strong and committed team. He is comfortable with his wife in the "lime light," and she respects his loving leadership. They are focused on working together for a common purpose, using the individual gifts and resources that God has given. Struggling over who leads and controls does not even seem to be an issue.

3. There was a clear and rapid progression from exposure to the message of redemption to becoming actively involved in God's redemptive work.

4. In the case of this couple, they were not just hearers of the words, but doers— acting proactively on what they learned (see James 1:22).

5. Aquila and Priscilla probably owned a large home, and perhaps had significant financial resources. They probably were unusually hospitable. They may have been strong leaders with an entrepreneurial style, in keeping with self-employed businesspeople. They evidently loved the Lord and His church with great passion and commitment.

6. They invested heavily in discipling Apollos, who clearly had significant gifts but incomplete knowledge of the faith.

7. They risked their lives in some way for Paul as his coworkers.

8. They continued to have a passionate and active ministry and care for people even as they grew older. The flames did not die out.

9. As a husband and wife grow closer to God, God will be at work refining and purifying each of them. As they become more and more godly, they will relate in deeper and more meaningful ways, more closely resembling the relationship within the Trinity.

10. Ideas: Ministering as a couple requires good communication. Ministry as a couple stimulates praying together. Ministry as a couple provides a common focus that requires shared time and conversation. It adds another level of value to the marriage because it is the platform for a work of God. It takes commitment and discipline to prioritize and invest time and energy in both family and ministry.

NOTES

ABOUT THE AUTHOR

Since 1977, Tommy Nelson has been the Pastor of Denton Bible Church, located in Denton, Texas. He has been featured on "Focus on the Family," "FamilyLife Today," "Josh McDowell," "For Faith and Family," and other national broadcasts.

In addition to the Song of Solomon materials, he is the author of three books: *The Book of Romance, The Big Picture: Understanding the Story of the Bible,* and *The Problem of Life with God.* He recently released a new audio/video series on Ecclesiastes entitled *A Life Well Lived.*

Tommy graduated from the University of North Texas with a Bachelor's Degree in Education. He then attended Dallas Theological Seminary in Dallas, Texas, where he received the Master of Arts in Biblical Studies degree.

Tommy has been married to Teresa Nelson for more than 30 years. They have two sons, one grandson, and one granddaughter.

ACKNOWLEDGEMENTS

Tommy Nelson and Serendipity House Publishing wish to thank the team of writers, editors, and designers that labored together to create this resource. Joe Snider and Ben Colter worked with Tommy Nelson to translate this content into a small-group experience. Other key contributors on the editorial team were: Ron Keck, Cathy Tardif, Rick Howerton, and Kathy Bence. Scott Lee provided art direction and many of the design elements. David Carlson of Studio Gear Box developed the cover design.

CREDITS

Serendipity and Tommy Nelson made use of the following resources in developing the Homework Series:

The Song of
Solomon Series
© 1995
Hudson Productions

Maximum Marriage
Series
© 2004
Tommy Nelson

HomeWorks Series

In a world that competes for nearly every minute of our time and energy while offering so many choices on how to order our lives, it's sometimes hard to figure out what works. Our homes, kids, careers, and even church life all have the potential to take us out of balance if not managed according to God's Word and instruction. Why is this important to us? Why should it be important to you? Because God is radically in love with His family. And He is radically in love with your family. *And because home still works.*

✠ *Some Assembly Required: Instructions for an Amazing Marriage*

✠ *Dream Team: The Power of Two*

✠ *Turning Up the Heat: Rekindle Romance and Passion*